Spells for Groovy Times

Kerri Connor, with Krystle Hope,
Cover by Alexis Hosta

Weed Witch Publishing LLC

About the Authors

Kerri Connor is the leader of The Gathering Grove, a family friendly earth based spiritual 501 (C) (3) nonprofit organization and has been practicing her craft since the 1980s. A graduate from the University of Wisconsin, Kerri earned a B.A. in Communications. Visit her online at www.KerriConnor.com to find links to all her social media. Kerri is an Aquarius.

Krystle Hope is a lover of coffee, grilled cheese, and horror movies. She was a contributing author on *Spells for Good Times* and *Conjuring with Cannabis*. Watch for her debut novel *BLOOD AND LIES*, a paranormal romance. Krystle is the host of Must Love Books podcast. You can find her on Instagram @krystlehope And @MustLoveBooksPodcast.

Other Books by Kerri Connor

- 420 Days of Weed Witchery: Spells, Rituals & Techniques to Enhance Your Practice (Llewellyn Publications 2025)

- Conjuring with Cannabis: Spells and Rituals for the Weed Witch (Llewellyn Publications 2023)

- 420 Meditations: Enhance Your Spiritual Practice with Cannabis (Llewellyn Publications 2021)

- Wake, Bake & Meditate: Take Your Spiritual Practice to a Higher Level with Cannabis (Llewellyn Publications 2020)

- Spells for Tough Times (Llewellyn Publications 2012)

Contents

Disclaimer

Using, distributing, growing, or selling cannabis is a federal crime and may be illegal in your state or local vicinity. It is your responsibility to understand all laws pertaining to the possession or use of cannabis. Neither the author nor publishers are accountable for consequences derived from the possession or use thereof.

Always seek the advice of a qualified health care provider regarding medical or mental health questions. This book is not a substitute for medical advice.

Introduction

Hello, friends and welcome to a groovy new age!

This book was originally written as *Spells for Good Times* when we were coming out of the worst pandemic seen in our lifetime. It has been revised, added to, and is now being released as *Spells for Groovy Times.*

These past several years have taught us the importance of caring for ourselves. They have taught us our mental, emotional, and spiritual health is just as important as our physical health – not only our individual health, but also as a society. They taught us if we do not care for one another, if we do not protect one another, we cannot survive as a society. Life has become somewhat heavy.

While every generation has faced difficulties, we have come to a point in America where I often find myself asking, *How does this get better? How do we find our way out of this mess we have created?*

The answer is, there is no easy way. Change, especially societal change, is difficult, and takes years. We know this from historical examples. Sadly, we have also seen the more things change, the more they stay the same. Fighting "the man" is too often a matter of survival, not betterment. Our systems are showing they are outdated, flawed, and filled with loop holes the unethical take advantage of. The only way for real change to be made is with radical innovative ideas instead of repeating the same tired old actions and expecting different results.

As witches, we can transform negative energy into positive energy, not only for ourselves, but for our communities and the future. This means we need to take an active part in building a brighter future for ourselves, our families, our communities, and our planet. Any action, and often the most important action we can take, begins with ourselves. The work we do on and for ourselves shines a light onto others.

Have you been bummed out? Has life been feeling like a drag? Are you ready to feel better about yourself and the world around you? Are you ready to take back your own power and use it to give yourself the happiness you want and deserve? Are you ready to start a path to a fab new groovier life?

We will use spells, rituals, affirmations, meditations, prayers, and journal writing to fight what bums us out while sending out vibes of positive energy. Let's promote love, happiness, and peace.

Now, don't get the wrong idea: we are fully aware it's not all, "Love and light makes the world go around!" Trust me, I know! But that isn't the point here. The point is the world has suffered. We are still suffering, but people are finding common ground with recent historical events which has let them know they are not alone. We have not only all felt pain, but we have also now recognized so much pain in others. For empaths, the past several years have been overwhelming. We can use what we have learned and what we have seen to make major decisions about how we want our lives to be in the future. The choice is truly up to each one of us. We can focus on the hate and fear that is still prevalent in our society, or we can focus on love and compassion, both for ourselves and others.

There are different theories about when the official Age of Aquarius began (or begins, as a few theories don't claim it is yet here). I am on the boat that the Great Conjunction, which took place in Aquarius on the Winter Solstice 2020, was the kickoff to this formidable new era. An Aquarius myself, this theory feels the truest to me. I have felt incredible energy shifts not only in the environment around me, but in myself too. This is our time. We can create the world we want. We can have equality for all. We can have peace. We can create a society that values life. We can create a society that values love and compassion and wisdom. But we must do the work to get there. It won't happen overnight, and it will most certainly will not be easy. Nothing worth having is. It will take work from all of us to create a more loving, more equitable future for all. We must start somewhere. We must be the beacons to light up the way. We must be the ones to push forward. We must make the changes we want to see. If not us, then who?

There is a great awakening happening. People are opening their eyes and seeing the old ways don't necessarily mean the right ways. Things are changing, and with these changes come problems. Not everyone wants progress. Not everyone wants a world filled with positivity and compassion. They do not want a world with equality. They still want a world with power and control resting in the hands of the few. With any luck, our created positivity will reach those who desperately need it.

Creating a loving, compassionate world begins with each one of us. Learning how to heal, how to bounce back, how to move forward can be a difficult path. It is where the real work lies. Being compassionate does not equate with being a pushover. This is another area where society seems to be getting it completely wrong. You are free and encouraged to not only love yourself and others, but you are also free to fight against the systems of injustice which try to hold people down. Fighting against injustice is one of the highest forms of compassion we have.

Healing may require professional assistance. This book is not a substitute for any situation which requires therapy. Magic should never be a replacement or substitute for therapy. It should always be in addition to the other work you do. We must always back up our magical work with work in the mundane world.

For those of you who are new to the Craft, the first chapter is an explanation of what magic is and how you can learn to use it to bring about a brighter future for yourself and others. After that we will dive right in. Feel free to either read this book straight through from beginning to end or go to the chapter you feel you need first, jumping around as you like. It is your practice, so do what works best for you.

If you are familiar with my other titles, you know I often write about cannabis in combination with magic. *Spells for Good Times* did not include weed witchery, but that will also be remedied here with additions made for those who partake in the Ganja Goddess.

We hope this book will help open your eyes, lift your spirit, and inspire you to create a radical new age!

Chapter 1
Witchy Basics

If you are new to magic, you most likely have questions. That's okay! We are going to start off with basics that will have you on your way to a far out new practice in no time at all. Even if you aren't new to magic, stick with us for this brief introduction to the Craft; you may still pick up something new to you.

The number one question people often want to know is what is magic? I have a definition I have used since 1986, and it works well for me. Magic is the intentional transformation of energy, not explained by current science. Everything around us is energy. Energy is the combination of vibration and information. Sometimes we can see it; sometimes we can't. When we cast spells, or even say a prayer, we are encouraging the energies of the universe to transform our wish into reality.

Let's think about it in scientific terms. We know that ice (a solid) vibrates slowly because it is a solid. The information it contains is water that is really cold. We can apply heat to the ice, and it will melt to water (a liquid) that vibrates more quickly. It is still water, but now it isn't as cold. If we apply more heat to the water, it will steam and break apart into the gases hydrogen and oxygen with extremely fast vibrations. We have transferred the energy of both hydrogen and oxygen by applying the energy of heat.

Magic works in a similar way. We transform energies with our intention to create a new reality. We have diverse types of energies we can choose from or, for best results, combine to support our intention.

Energy

Energy is all around us. It is in everything that surrounds us. It runs through us, and we too, are a part of energy. Different parts of our world and existence consists of diverse types of energy. We can tap into these different energy types to use in our magic for mind blowing results.

There are four major types of energy that exist. Different traditions may teach different classifications of energies or the type of energies in those classifications. The following is the method I use, particularly when discussing generalities. If you are part of a specific tradition, feel free to use energy the way your tradition teaches, but don't skip over this section. You may find something you like, and it never hurts to learn how others work their magic.

The first type of energy is your own personal life force. Everything about you is energy. Both your physical and spiritual bodies consist of this energy. It is the energy you have the most control over and therefore can use and direct the most effectively once you learn how. If you work with chakras, auras, or channels in the body, these are all a part of your own personal life force. We decide if we want to share our energies with others or not and can put up protective energetic barriers if needed. Think about how your energy affects others without you even really trying. Give a smile to someone who needs it, and you can feel their spirits rise. A stern, angry, hard stare, can give someone goosebumps and raise their hair. These are simple forms of energy we give off without even thinking about it. What can we do, then, when we we really put our mind and our energy into it?

The next type of energy comes from the earth. There are several energy types that fall into the earth energy category. The first type can be felt through ley lines and sacred sites. Sacred sites include places such as famous henges, springs, or wells, but also include the sacred sites you create yourself. At The Gathering Grove, we have a few sacred sites: The Inner Grove Ritual Area, The Other Grove Community Ritual Area, and The Spiral Labyrinth. These area of the land have been used for decades for spiritual purposes. This consistent constant spiritual use has created its own distinct energy to the land – an energy that we and others can use when needed.

Earth energy also includes the energies of the elements and their counterparts. This means the energies of air, fire, water, and earth. We often add these energies to our spell work. Herbs, resins, oils, flowers, stones, crystals, and moon water are all a part of earth energies, each with their own corresponding intentions. This also includes frequencies and sound waves – the simple act of chanting sends energy outward as sound waves.

The third type of energy we work with is the energy of our deities, angels, and spirit guides. This energy can be known as "divine energy," "ethereal energy," or "spiritual energy." When we call upon a deity in prayer, ritual, or spellwork, we are asking for this type of energy to work with our intention to help it become a reality.

The last type of energy we use is known as "celestial" or "cosmic energy" and incorporates the energies from the sun, moon, and stars. Part of this energy is rolled into your zodiac sign. This is the energy we tap into when we work with the phases of the moon. This type of energy encompasses the different energies from space.

We can combine different types of energies together to push towards our goals. For example, a spell using incense, chants, and dance on a full moon around a bonfire built with woods corresponding to your intention is a good way to cover several energy bases. Add in some weed, for a psychedelic trip. The more energies we incorporate, the more powerful our working becomes. This isn't to say you must have a huge list of ingredients. Your own energy and your own intention will always be your strongest energy, but the other energies combined do give your workings a boost. The ceremony of certain spellwork or ritual allows you to enter a state where you can direct and use your energy in a magical manner more efficiently. You need to experiment and see what works best for you. I love to incorporate various aspects into my spell work – sometimes. And sometimes I just want something fast, easy, and straight to the point. What works for you one day might not be what you are looking for another day. That is okay. It is your magical *practice*.

Because our magical wants and needs fluctuate, each of the other sections in this book will have a variety of diverse ways to tackle the same type of problem. This way, you can use what you need, when you need it. A ritualized spell working can be backed up with daily affirmations and journal writings. Or a journal writing may lead you to start a daily affirmation to build up to a ritualized spell working. We learn differently. We act differently. We perform our magic differently. I simply cannot emphasize enough the importance of doing what works for you. Within reason, of course.

Journal Exercise

Think about the types of energy. How do you currently use these energies? What energy/ies would you like to incorporate more into your spiritual or magical practice?

Recognize Your Power

Your energy gives you the power to change your environment. To achieve your full power, you must first recognize your own energy. This can be far more difficult than what people realize because we are often detached from ourselves. To work magic successfully, you must learn to use your own energy and power. The first step in learning to use them is to learn how to recognize them.

Let's start with these easy experiments to see what I mean.

Begin by visualizing yourself when you are hurt. What body language do you give off? What facial muscles do you use? Where do you hold tension in your body? Picture in your mind what you look like when you have been hurt. Look into a mirror if it helps you. Set this image in your mind's eye. Once you see yourself and how you look, project the image outside of yourself. Fix the same look on your face and project it outward. Tighten the muscles where you would hold the tension. Feel it as if it is there weighing you down. Put yourself into your visualization and feel yourself project that energy outward.

Once you feel yourself enter this state, walk up to people you know and gauge their reactions. Do they notice the energy you are sending out? Do they notice you are down? You are giving off this energy to those around you. They should feel it. Some people will respond to your energy by feeling down themselves. Others may send you a boost of positive energy to not only help you, but to counteract the lower vibration you are sending out to protect themselves.

Do this experiment again by visualizing yourself as happy and energetic. When you see yourself this way, you allow it to happen. Think of a time when you were extra happy. Visualize that moment. Put yourself in it again and tap into the energy you felt then. Carry that energy forward with you to the present and again project it out to those around you. How do they react?

You can easily project emotional energies such as happiness or sadness or even anger. These are energies that we work with frequently without even realizing it. We often receive energies too without noticing, which in turn can affect the energies we give off to others.

Pay attention to the energies you see and feel other people sending off. Do they appear to be aware they are giving their energy away? Do they know the status of their energy? Is it a positive, uplifting energy or a negative, downtrodden one?

This exercise shows us how easily we flip the switch on and off while turning the dial throughout the day, everyday. Every day we decide what energy we are willing to show and what energy we are willing to receive in our normal interactions. Often though, we do not pay conscious attention to what we are sending or receiving. We are all guilty of it from time to time. This can lead to habits, and usually not the best ones at that. We often let in and send out far more negativity than we mean to, as we do not know how to properly block it in the first place, much less ground it or convert it to positivity. This book will help you change that.

Each one of us can walk into a room filled with people and use our energy to either boost the mood or dampen it. This exercise also shows how powerful your energy is without you even trying. If you can change the energy of a room without much effort, think what you can do once you understand how to work with the different energies available to you.

Your next step is to pay attention to your energy shifts by spending time throughout your day checking in with the energy you are sending into your environment. Are you radiating positive or negative energy? If you find yourself sending out negative energy, what can you do to shift it to the positive side? Not sure? That is okay, as it part of what this book is about – adjusting or converting energy from negative to positive.

Journal Exercise

Keep an energy journal throughout the day for two weeks. Set reminder alarms or notifications for random times each day. When your alarm goes off, check your energy. Where is it? Learning to pay attention to your energy helps you to learn to control your energy. This is important for learning how to use other energies later. Since your own energy is your greatest power, learning to control, focus, and direct it is of the upmost importance when performing magic. Magic simply won't work correctly without the proper energy behind it.

Flipping the Switch

We are made of energy. We can send it and receive it from others, and we can use it to alter our environment. So how do we do it on purpose?

Let's go back to our example with water in its different stages of matter: solid, liquid, and gas. In that scenario, we applied an outside energy source to to the water. That energy source was heat. When a new energy source is applied, change happens.

When we do magic, we are the main energy source. We have the option to use the other types of energy discussed earlier to back up our work and to add more power to it, but our life energy is the main energy source we use. We are the heat in the water example.

We perform magic by learning to control, focus, and direct our energy into creating a desired change or outcome. We take in energy from around us, convert it to our will, and send it back out into the universe. The backup sources we use contribute their energies according to their associated correspondences.

We convert energy in unusual ways – through spell work, ritual, meditation, prayers, and affirmations. Each of these workings has its own benefits and situations it is best suited for, and each requires its own set of skills. When we combine these skills together, we influence energies with our desires, and magic happens.

Skills of the Craft

While there are many important skills to utilize in your Craft, including patience, visualization is one of your most essential skills. When you visualize something happening, particularly with an energy shift, you help to make the shift happen. Visualization helps us learn to control, focus, and direct our energies to create the changes we seek.

Is visualization really that important? Yes! This cannot be emphasized enough. And yet, I understand that visualization can be a huge problem for people, which is why I want to cover this skill first. Let's talk a bit about the issues with visualization that people face and discuss ways of overcoming them.

When someone tells me, "Just imagine," I do. I do because my brain is wired to allow me to. The problem is, not everyone's brain is wired the same, and not everyone has had the same experiences to draw from. So, someone tells me imagine a mountain, and I can suddenly find myself in the Grand Tetons staring out over Jenny Lake. I can smell the fresh air and the pine trees on the breeze. I can hear the cranes calling along with a chipmunk rustling in the leaves. I have also been to the Grand Tetons, where I was able to stare out over Jenny Lake, smell the air, and hear the cranes. This makes visualizing it easy for me. I can quickly and easily put myself back into a place I have been before.

For some people, being told to imagine a mountain sends their brain into overdrive. It doesn't bring up just one mountain. It brings up dozens of different images: the Rocky Mountains, the Smoky Mountains, the Alps, Mount Everest, Superstition Mountain and more. Then the brain wants to decide which mountain works the best and begins an argument with itself as it goes through the pros and cons of each one.

Other people do not have experience with mountains and therefore have a challenging time drawing on any inspiration to base their imagined mountain on. They can't fully visualize it because they do not have the required information to draw upon.

These are issues that can be overcome with prep work before completing your workings. Always read your spell or meditation first. Remember – the Craft is a practice; we can *practice* all we want. We can practice performing a spell before we perform it for real. We can practice a ritual or meditation before we perform it. Practicing ahead of time allows us to find where issues might exist – needed supplies, pronunciation problems, visualization limitations – and correct them ahead of time. We want our magic to work, and to ensure it does, we need to be able to perform it with confidence. The first few times you try something new, your confidence level may not be the greatest, that's okay. Practice allows us to build our confidence and deal with any roadblocks that may be in the way.

If you come across something you don't know how to pronounce or aren't sure how to visualize a concept, remember, research is your friend. Search engines can tell you how to pronounce things with a query asking for the pronunciation. When you aren't sure how to visualize something, you can also do searches for images and videos. A little bit of research can help your visualizations and workings in a big way.

When you feel your visualizations may not be the strongest, there is another way to give your working a boost and that is by using your own symbolism. If there are times when you simply cannot visualize something, don't try to visualize it so specifically. Give it a more generic symbolism. For example, often with physical healing work, or any work that takes place inside the body, it might not be the best to visualize the exact process even if you can. Most people do not have the necessary medical knowledge to fully visualize what the inside of the body truly looks like, and other people may find even attempting to visualize their insides disturbing. Nothing wrong with that; it's your own personal preference, which needs to be respected.

There are ways you can use abstract symbolism to help you in these visualizations. For example, bones do not have to be seen as real bone with muscle attached; they can seen as made of steel or titanium with a robotic appeal. They can be seen as glass with a fragile quality that needs to be strengthened; perhaps the glass bones are visualized as being dipped into vibranium and hardened. What you picture in your mind is important, but it is even more important for you to understand what it means to you. The emphasis is on what it stands for.

These types of visualizations are also important for energy work, as most people don't physically see the energy with which they are working, with their eyes. You can visualize it in your mind's eye in a manner meaningful to you. Use colored light to represent energy, with assorted colors to represent distinct types.

What matters the most when you are using an abstract type of visualization in another extremely important skill of the Craft – your intention.

Intention is why you are doing a working. Focusing your intention with details builds not only the strength of your intention but also your confidence in your working. Your working is nothing without your intention.

Combine intention with visualization, add in energy and patience, and you have the basic ingredients for all sorts of wonderful magical workings. These are the basics of the Craft, and throughout the rest of this book we will talk about ways of using and combining them to create the futures and world you want to live in.

Journal Exercise

Throughout your workings, keep track of what you do, how you do it, and what outcome you receive. Write down pertinent information in your journal. If you choose to, you may copy things into your Book of Shadows later.

Self-Sabotage

No amount of magical work will change anything for the better if the work you do in the mundane world is counterproductive. This is a simple cold, hard truth. We cannot do magical work and then sabotage it with what we do in the mundane world and expect our magical work to be the victor. It doesn't work that way. Our magical work must always be backed up with supportive work in the mundane world. We are all guilty of screwing up, so when you do, step back, realize your mundane actions are in competition with your magical workings, and adjust. Don't beat yourself up. Turn yourself around and get back on track.

Whenever you do magical workings, think about how you will back it up with your nonmagical workings. Wanting to be a happier person with a bright future is wonderful, but it can be easier to say than to achieve.

We all have traumas, and to become our best, most complete, happiest self, we must deal with those traumas. We will discuss this more in the chapter on shadow work. For now, remember trauma responses can cause us to self-sabotage without realizing it. The more we heal trauma, the more effective our mundane workings are in backing up our magical workings. We must pay close attention to the actions we take in the mundane world to ensure they are supportive of our magic.

If you want a life that is more positive, groovier, you must be willing to make the changes required to bring the positivity in and keep the negativity out. Making minor changes at a time is easier to work into a routine than trying to do too much at once. As you successfully make changes, your self-esteem and confidence grow. Trying to make substantial changes all at once may be setting the bar too high. This results in self-sabotage by setting yourself up for failure. Give yourself the advantage of achieving successes by giving yourself more, smaller goals, instead of fewer, larger ones.

When things are tough, break it down into smaller more manageable parts. Instead of worrying about the month ahead, focus on the week ahead, or the day ahead, or even the hour ahead. Being mindful of your present helps create success.

Ethics and Responsibilities

I am not here to tell you which ethics system to subscribe to. What I will tell you is most do have certain aspects in common – most importantly, the concept of treating others how you yourself would like to be treated.

Some pathways promise a punishment to what you send out, others do not. Some say your punishment will be worse than what you send out. Some say your punishment will come in your next life. Some consider it consequences, and for others the idea of punishment is unheard of.

Whatever path you walk, whether it is structured or your own personal eclectic mix, you will have your own set of ethics and responsibilities you subscribe to.

Whatever you believe, remember, it is your belief. It is what you have chosen to affirm as your truth. Know what it is you are willing to stand by. Responsibilities are often overlooked while rights are celebrated. Do not forget about the responsibilities of your path, no matter what your path is. Following the ethical and responsibility guidelines of your individual pathway is part of where your spiritual power comes from. Think about it: if you say you believe in something but don't walk the walk, your credibility goes down. When your credibility goes down, so does your power. I am not referring to your credibility with others; this is your credibility withing yourself. You know when you are not living up to your own ideals, and when you aren't, you feel it. It weighs you down.

Stand by what you believe in. Live it. But also remember your beliefs are never set in stone and can be replaced with new ones. The more we learn, the more our beliefs change. This is enlightenment.

Journal Exercise

Evaluate your ethics and responsibilities. What do you believe in? Document your beliefs in your Book of Shadows.

Chapter 2
Flower Power

Spells for Groovy Times wouldn't be complete without adding in the magical power of the cannabis flower.

Weed Witchery allows the practitioner the benefits of both magic and cannabis. It is a beneficial plant rich with possibilities.

Weed (in any form of THC: edibles, concentrates, etc.) is a spiritual ally. It aids in shifting to the viewpoint of your higher self, it is a powerful entheogen, and broadens your imagination and creativity resulting in improved visualization, stronger magic, and better results.

My book *Conjuring with Cannabis* is a great guide for getting started in adding weed to your witchcraft practice. It:

- helps you get started with cleansing and blessing your equipment.

- offers magic for growers.

- teachers how to blend cannabis with other smokeable herbs.

- encourages the use of cannabis in spells to better yourself.

- explores using cannabis with shadow work.

My book *420 Days of Weed Witchery* helps you fully incorporate cannabis into your daily life, not only as an entheogen and aid, but also as an ingredient in your workings. If you are a cannabis user and want to learn more and fully incorporate it into your practice, please add them to your library.

Since I have already written a couple of books on weed, it will not be the main focus here, however there is some basic information I do want to include.

How Weed Hits

Cannabis, like any other plant, has its own correspondences. It can be used magically for:

- drawing or representing abundance and prosperity.

- bindings (especially the ash).

- cleansing negative energies.

- spirit communication.

- honoring and accepting death.

- healing of all kinds.

- hexing (especially the ash).

- drawing, representing, and honoring love.

- amplifying your magic.

- manifesting your desires.

- peaceful meditation.

- protection.

- restful sleep.

- an aphrodisiac and powerful additive for sex magic.

Strains also have their own individual correspondences. How does the strain make you feel? Happy? Calm? Excited? Energetic? Whatever effects the strain has on you, it corresponds with those qualities. This holds true for any negative effects you experience to. Keep track of how specific strains make you feel either in a weed journal or in your Book of Shadows.

When cannabis is used as an ingredient in spell work, you can tap into its energetic correspondences by using parts of the plant other than the flower. If you have access, leaves are a perfect substitution leaving the bud for you to smoke.

Hemp products also add some of the qualities of cannabis to your workings. Hemp paper, hemp twine, and hemp material or clothing, can all be incorporated into your practice.

Embrace the Power of the Flower

Getting stoned before meditating and visualization can help you lower walls, step into your higher point of view, connect with Spirit or Deity, and boost your imagination, creativity, or focus.

Getting stoned before spell or ritual work also aids you in connection with the universal force around you, boosting your connection, your power, and overall success.

Any of the workings in this book can be enhanced by adding cannabis either through consumption or as an ingredient representing its magical correspondences.

The spiritual benefits of working with weed have been experienced for thousands of years. Ancient people knew what worked based on trial and error and their experiences hold as proof to the power of cannabis. Today, we also learn through trial and error of what works best for us depending on our needs.

If you wish, incorporate weed into your practice in whatever way makes you most comfortable.

Journal Exercise

If you partake, write about your experience with weed. How do you currently use it in your life? How can you further incorporate it into your spirituality?

Chapter 3
Everyday Morning Magic

Some days you are excited to get out of bed and start the day. Other days, maybe not so much. Lying in bed when you first awaken in the morning is a wonderful place to start your magical workings. If you are someone who likes to hit the snooze button, you can fit in workings between alarms. If you don't already use a snooze on your alarm, you may want to start if you want to ensure you don't fall back asleep and to set time limits on these early morning workings.

Getting out of bed can sometimes feel like one of the most difficult things to do, particularly when depression has a hand in guiding your actions. The good news is, often once we do get moving, it gets easier to move. This is true from both emotional and physical standpoints. Habits kick in once we start moving. Some days you may feel like you are on autopilot. That's okay. We can work with that. For people who have a tough time physically, getting out of bed due to medical issues, often the limitations become less with movement. The key is to get moving. Beginning your magical work while still in bed gives you the opportunity to start your day off on an extra positive note.

Say Hello to the Day

How do you normally start your day? Does an alarm blare to wake you from your slumber? While of course I comprehend the reasoning behind obnoxious, loud sounds to pull us from our sleep, is there a better way to wake up?

I can remember the days I used to wake up reaching my arm out to feel for the alarm clock and hit the snooze button, often missing it so it would take several tries. I am not what one would call a morning person. With today's technology, I can simply tell my alarm to stop or snooze. I can also use that same technology to help me start my day off on the right foot by not using an alarm that resembles what I would hear if the house were on fire. Think about it – is a sound that is jarring and sets you on edge the best way to start your day? Not if you are looking to have more positive experiences in your life.

Whether you use a phone or other device for an alarm, you can choose from all kinds of different sounds to wake up with. Assistant devices allow you to set up an entire morning routine when your alarm goes off. In this way, you can allow your device to guide you through your routine.

Even without an interface to assist, you can create a morning routine to follow each day. Let's look at examples of both types or morning routines and then we can get into specifics on setting up your own.

My morning alarm on my Alexa device plays chimes at an increasing volume. It doesn't jerk me awake; it lets me wake up more slowly and gradually, allowing for moments in the between-world of the waking and the sleeping. When I say good morning, I can be given a morning affirmation, followed by a meditative song in which I can work with the affirmation. I can take in a quick meditation and finish with my daily horoscope and weather report. All before opening my eyes if I wish. Some people may find this idea atrocious, but for me, it is a much gentler way of waking up than the startling clang of an alarm.

Without the assistance of an interface, you may still be able to try several types of alarms to chose from. There are clocks available on the market that have much gentler alarm sounds than the standard. It's amazing how something as simple as the sound of what you wake up to can have influence on your day. At the same time, it also makes perfect sense to not start the morning off by scaring yourself awake. You can choose an uplifting song to use as an alarm. Music is a powerful tool for setting a mood. We will use it often in this book.

Once you wake, you can perform one of the following morning meditations, repeat an affirmation, or both before you get out of bed. You obviously won't be doing a full spell or ritual before getting out of bed each day, but there are activities you can do to help start your day off on a positive note as soon as you wake.

Journal Exercise

Pay attention to your regular morning routine. How do you wake up each day? How do you feel immediately upon waking? Document your morning activities and feelings. Add in the changes you want to make to your morning routine. If you change your alarm sound, what do you change it from and to? If you are someone who has a challenging time adjusting to change, only make one change at a time and give it a few days before adding in another. For example, begin by changing your alarm. After several days, add in a morning affirmation. After several more days, add in a morning meditation. Document the changes you make and reflect on how they change your outlook for the day.

Affirmation of the Day

Read this list of affirmations and pick which you want to use. Try:

- writing them down on index cards or in a journal kept next to your bed for easy morning access.

- a small dry erase board to write daily affirmations on.

- program a digital device to wake you up with your chosen affirmation.

What do you want to focus on? What do you need to focus on?

Healing Emotional Trauma

- Each new day is a new beginning. Today is a new beginning.

- My life is under my control.

- I make the most of each day given to me. I am blessed.

- I am strong. I am loved. I am at peace.

- I invite health, wealth, and happiness into my life.

- I use boundaries when and where necessary.

- I release that which does not serve me.

- I am healing. I am strong. I am loved,

- I bring strength, curiosity, and hope into each day.

- I welcome peace and kindness into my life.

Building Confidence

- I accept myself for who I am. I am right where I should be.

- Today is the first day of the rest of my life. Each day is a new beginning, a fresh start.

- I claim this day as my own. It is mine to make the most of.

- I am brave. I am strong. I am fearless.

- I am the best me I can be.

- Today my light will shine.

- Today I will be confident and joyful.

- I make room for new opportunities.

- I am free to be me.

- I am all that I am meant to be.

Shift Your Perspective

- I rise with the sun. Bright and ready for my day.

- I look forward to what the day may bring.

- As I breathe in, as I breathe out, I prepare for the day ahead.

- I am confident in myself and ready for what the day will bring.

- I am ready for any challenge set before me today.

- As I awaken for the day, I awaken my mind to new experiences.

- I let go of my sleep and prepare for a new day of learning and loving.

- I start my day with an open heart and an open mind.

- I welcome abundance into my life. I welcome in joy.

- Today I will spread the joy of me.

Encouraging Self-Love

- I stand on the side of love. Love for myself, love for others.

- Today I will care for me. Today I will do my best for me.

- I welcome each new day I am given.

- I am happy with myself. I am the perfect me.

- I am blessed. I am whole. I am complete.

- I accept myself for who I am. I love myself for who I am.

- I live to love – myself, others, the world.

- I was made to be me. I am who I am.

- I live my truth, today and every day.

- I trust myself. I have faith in who I am.

Enlightenment, Choosing a Spiritual Life

- I choose the path before me. My steps are my own.

- As I open my eyes, I open my mind to a new day.

- Today I welcome love and joy into my life.

- Today I embrace happiness and love.

- I am positive. I am at peace. I am love.

- I honor love and life.

- I am a part of the whole. The universe is not complete without me.

- I walk my path with grace, through all twists and turns.

- I honor the light within me.

- I am filled with love – love for myself and love for others.

Affirmations are the perfect way to set an intention for the day.

Morning Meditations

Starting off with a quick morning meditation gives you the chance to fully set the tone and intention for your day. Giving yourself the few minutes it takes for a brief meditation is an act of self-love. In this section, you will find brief meditations you can do before leaving your bed. You can do these on your own or in combination with an affirmation. If you can, add cheery, uplifting music without having to leave your bed. Earphones kept next to the bed can prevent bothering a sleeping partner. Plan on what meditation you would like to do the night before and read it to get yourself familiar with it. Leave yourself a note next to the bed or a digital reminder to help you perform your meditation in the morning until you are set in the routine.

Using a snooze feature lets you perform a morning meditation before leaving bed without having to worry about falling back to sleep, and of course this give you the opportunity to set the snooze for the amount of time you want. Five to ten minutes for one of these meditations is sufficient.

Gentle Wake Up Meditation

We have been programmed to believe jumping out of bed, slapping off the alarm, and barreling full steam ahead is the only ideal way to wake up each day. There is no one size fits all in anything, including how we wake and start our day. It's not a race. Chill out and take the time you need to get yourself ready for the day, and that includes spending a few moments to allow yourself to wake from your slumber in a more gentle, mellow way.

After you wake, close your eyes again and allow yourself to slip into the liminal time between sleeping and waking, We often call this "resting our eyes." The intention isn't to fall asleep, but it isn't to be overly conscious either. This in-between time has its own magic. It is as if we are in both places at once, and yet in neither. Take the opportunity to not only notice this special time but allow yourself to become at one with it. It may feel like a waking dream to you. Allow yourself to be only in the present moment – neither totally awake nor asleep.

When you are ready, slowly being to become aware of your surroundings. If you are using a snooze alarm, nature sounds, wind chimes or another simple and serene sound is a perfect way to announce it is time to become aware of your surroundings. Consciously, yet gently, pull or shift yourself from the in-between space to the waking world. No need for a blaring alarm screaming at you for you to get out of bed. A gentle, easy shift allows you to start your day without a startling experience. No anxiety from the sudden change from sleep to awake. No panic at a loud sudden sound. Just a gentle shift from one magical existence to another – though the second is a bit more concrete.

Taking these few extra moments to acknowledge and experience the magic of the in-between sleep and waking liminal time also helps teach us how to recognize other moments when magic shifts us to an in-between space or time.

Body Scan Meditation

This meditation is particularly good for people who suffer from any type of chronic pain no matter what the source of the pain is, and those of us who are slow to fully awake. Getting up too quickly without being sure your body is ready for movement can cause vertigo, dizziness or falls. In this meditation, you will focus on only the physical aspects of your body: a scan to see how everything is feeling and to give yourself a heads-up as to what you may be dealing with before you start to move around. A body that is moved when it isn't ready can suffer unexpected sprains, strains, or cramps. A quick meditative check-in can help avoid mishaps.

With your eyes closed, begin with your toes. Slowly wiggle them back and forth. Curl them tightly, hold for a few seconds, and release. Flex your feet, rotate your ankles, tighten your calves and let them all relax. Is everything okay so far? If you come across anything that hurts, any areas that are tender, achy, or tense, make a mental note on where you need extra care. Don't make any judgments about the pain, only note it is there and that it may need special attention later. Bend your knees, leaving your feet flat on the bed. Let your knees fall to the side, first to the left, then to the right. Allow your feet to slide back down the bed, straightening your legs into a comfortable position.

Focus on your abdomen. Tighten and release your core muscles, inspecting the results as you continue to travel upward through your body. Make your hands into tight fists, relax, stretch your fingers apart as far as you can, and relax again. Raise your shoulders toward your ears, relax. Rotate your head left, then right. Relax. Bend your arms, folding them around yourself for a gentle hug. Hold yourself for a moment as you tighten and release your facial muscles.

Make note of any place you need to be careful with or any pains you need to attend to once you are ready to get out of bed,. Take deep, calming breaths, release your self-hug, and open your eyes.

Bright New Day Meditation

As I have grown older, my views on summer days have completely changed from when I was a child. Back then, I couldn't stand the sunlight shining into my bedroom window because it would wake me up so early. Now, however, I have a much deeper appreciation for the sunlight that streams through my windows. With the way my house is situated, I often don't close my eastern bedroom curtains, so the sun comes in as soon as it begins breaking through the trees. What used to be aggravating to me, is now inviting instead. The sun coming through my window is often my favorite part of the morning particularly when accompanied by cat snuggles.

This meditation is to help you capture the energy of the sunrise and hold it in your power throughout the day.

Before you open your eyes, begin your meditation by recalling an image of just before dawn. The sun has not yet broken the horizon, but the colors of twilight are glowing. You know that the sunrise you are about to see will be spectacular. Perhaps the sunrise you expect to see may be a moment you have previously experienced that you found to be profound or meaningful and would like to relive. If you haven't personally seen a sunrise that strongly spoke to you, that is okay. Is there an image you have seen in a movie, on TV, in a photograph, in a painting, or from somewhere else you can draw to mind a particularly brilliant, bright sunrise?

Focus on the moment right before the sun breaks the horizon line. The colors of the sky around you changes. It begins to lighten, a little more, a little more, and then the first rays break over the horizon. Focus on the colors you see. Feel the rays of the sun as they reach out to warm your skin. Follow the sunrise in your mind for several minutes, allowing it to rise to the ideal image for you. Soak in the heat, the energy, and the power of the sun. Feel the light as it reaches and blends with your energetic field. Visualize the light charging you like a solar battery. Take in the light and energy storing it throughout all of you. Fill yourself with as much light as you can. Let it wash over you, warm you, and charge you.

Hold on to this feeling for a moment in silence. You can store this light, this energy, and carry it with you for the rest of the day. When you are ready, open your eyes.

If you need a pick-me-up during the day, simply close your eyes for a moment, recall the image and feeling, then allow that burst of energy to release and give yourself a boost.

Slay the Day Meditation

Some days, you know you are going to have a tough day ahead of you, which can make getting out of bed a bit more difficult. This meditation is for those days. Empower and prepare yourself before ever leaving your bed by ensuring you see yourself as conquering whatever obstacles may stand in your way.

If necessary, set your snooze, timer, or other alarm. If you would like to play music along with this meditation, be sure to have it prepared ahead of time.

With your eyes closed, take deep breaths. Instead of focusing on what obstacles you must deal with today, set those aside and instead focus on seeing yourself in a strong, positive image. You may choose whatever image of strength you want to emulate. You can be a superhero, a knight in shining armor, a powerful witch or wizard, a Transformer, or a God. Think indestructible. Unbeatable. You can channel the energy of whatever you want. You can be whatever, whoever, you want. It is your choice. Take on the added strength from your visualization. How can you incorporate this strength into helping you today? How can it help you overcome and complete the challenges that lie in front of you? Remember, you can visualize your challenges with symbolism instead of a more literal visualization. Do what works for you and allows you to see yourself slaying any obstacle in your way.

Have fun with this meditation. Be creative and let your imagination run wild. Today, nothing can stop you. You are full of confidence. The day is yours. You are a powerhouse. Pump yourself up, build the energy in your mind. Focus it on slaying the day and begin directing your energy when you are ready by opening your eyes.

Get Trippy Meditation

One of my favorite ways to wake up in the morning is to imagine I am starting the day off with a romp through a giant field of dandelions, no one else in sight. Completely free with my spirit running wild. Sometimes I may imagine my old dog trotting along at my side. Other times I am a feral warrior child. This is my safe place. This is where I ran as a child to escape and recharge. This is where I drew energy from long before I knew I was doing it.

Find your safe place. Find the place which cleanses you and recharges you.

Before you get out of bed in the morning, take a trip there to begin your day.

Journal Exercise

Evaluate your morning routine every couple of weeks. What changes have you made and what affects have you noticed? Continue making any adjustments you desire and continue checking in with yourself for occasional re-evaluations.

Theme Songs and the Soundtrack of Life

Music is a radical tool. The sound of it can instantly bring back memories; it can transport you to a different time and place. It can help you sleep and help you wake up. It is as ideal with gentle meditation as it is with active exercise. It can help you feel empowered, or mellow. It can boost your confidence. When life is a drag, it can raise your spirits. It can help to mend a broken heart.

Do you have a theme song for your life? Music lovers will often already have one picked out. Your theme song is a song that can either touch or represent you deeply. You feel you could have written it yourself. It speaks to you on a more personal level than most other music. Theme songs may change over time, or you may add new titles to your theme song collection; you may have many theme songs on your soundtrack of life. As life goes on and you grow and evolve, you might set an entire soundtrack aside and conduct a new symphony to take its place.

Using theme songs and playlists is a straightforward way to add the energy from sound waves to your workings, and to give even mundane tasks a hint of magic. Music contains the energy put into its making. It also triggers an energy response in the listener. Let it. These energies combine, allowing them to grow and become stronger. The energy from music can feed the energy of your personal life force. Adding music to your workings, no matter what type they are, adds and allows you to increase desired energy.

If you use cannabis, you are probably well aware of the effects of being high when listening to music. Tap into this and use it when you can. An out of the world musical high creates mind blowing energetic power.

As a part of Gen X, I can attest to how much easier it is to have music accompany your life these days than it has been before. The digital age and streaming services not only make music instantly and conveniently available at your fingertips, but they are also responsible for giving musicians a broader market, and for connecting listeners to a much larger array of talent. With music as accessible as it is now, it would be a shame to not tap into this energy source and use it for your benefit.

Spend time exploring music and creating playlists to help you in your magical workings. There are several types of playlists you may want to have in your library. Topic titles include:

- Morning Meditations

- Morning Routines

- Sleep Meditations

- Bedtime Routines

- Empowerment Songs

- Energy Raising Songs

- Chill Lounge for Relaxing

- Workout Playlist

- Songs to Make Me Smile

There are others you can make of course, but these are the basics for your musical treasury. Make the lists you need. Using music in your practices is like lighting a candle, in the sense that both the music and candle are tools you can use to help achieve your overall goal. Instead of storing this set of tools in a wooden chest or placing them on an altar, you store them on a device or the cloud.

I often listen to other people's playlists or streaming stations while I am working as background music, then when a new song I like comes on, I can easily add it to the appropriate playlist or lists. I love how easy it is to incorporate music into every aspect of my day.

Music services offer the "if you like this, then you may like this" feature. Use it! This is another fantastic way to discover new music that speaks to you.

Remember, anything you do can be made more magical, more powerful, more intense, more energetic, more somber, more of whatever you want it to be, by adding music to it.

Journal Exercise

What role has music previously played in your spiritual practice? What are your musical tastes? How can you incorporate music more into your practice?

Stretch and Be Active

Studies have shown that being active helps to put people into a happier, more positive mood. [1] The problem is, it's also easier to be active when you are already in a happier, more positive mood. You must take the first step to get the ball rolling; once you start moving, you start producing more endorphins, which make you feel better and make you feel like being more active.

Begin your day with simple stretches. Take the time to really check in with your body by focusing on the muscles in use with each stretch you perform. Begin while in bed if you like, working your way into a sitting position, and then finally into standing.

If you have chronic pain, inflammation, joint, or other issues; stretching allows your body to start activating and gives you a heads-up on where issues may be lurking, Not only do you know what part of your body to be more cautious with, you have locations to start sending healing energy. Those without chronic pain still benefit from the slow stretching approach to getting out of bed since it is another way to practice the mind and body connection.

If you are not used to being active, there are easy ways to begin that are less strenuous but allow you to build intensity into your practice as you are ready to level up. Yoga, in it's variety of forms, and walking are both low-impact and low intensity ways to add in activity. As you progress, your skills, stamina, and strength will too. Build yourself up

---

1. Felipe B. Schuch, Davy Vancampfort, Joseph Firth, et al., "Physical Activity and Incident Depression: A Meta-Analysis of Prospective Cohort Studies," *American Journal of Psychiatry* 175, no, 7 (July 2018): 631-648, https://doi.org/10.1176/appi.ajp.2018.17111194.

to a minimum of twenty minutes of activity a day. If it's easier to do it all at once, great! If not, you can break it up throughout the day.

Being physically active and allowing your body to produce endorphins is an important way to back up your magical workings with your mundane workings. The more you move, the more endorphins you produce, the happier your body can keep you. Your body is designed to make you feel good and give you pleasure. Using the biological tools your body has to improve positive feelings is the most natural type of magic there is. When something makes you truly feel good, do it.

Activity and exercise also build energy you can use magically. Use this energy to send intentions into the universe. Adding affirmations while building energy, such as with dance or drumming, is an excellent way to quickly boost positivity. Combining magical and mundane tasks together is key to being successful in creating a brighter future. They go together hand in hand.

Mornings set the tone for the day. Work to create a routine that leaves you feeling refreshed, invigorated, and ready for whatever adventures lie ahead.

Journal Exercise

Analyze your current morning routine and find the things you do out of habit that may not have a beneficial result. Replacing habits helps us achieve our goals. For example, what is something you do now that you can replace with exercise? For many, it's time watching TV. If you like to watch the news in the morning, do exercises along with it. Record how you feel both before and after your workout Can you feel the increase in endorphins as they boost your mood?

Chapter 4
Go with the Flow

Showering and bathing are acts of cleansing not only physically, but also emotionally, mentally, and spiritually. This makes the shower or bathtub a suitable place for morning spell work that is designed to wash away any negativity and boost your mood and energy level. In this section, you will learn ways to refresh and recharge yourself with easy spell work to perform in your shower or tub.

Prepare your ingredients ahead of time so they are already to go when you need them. Running around trying to pull ingredients together in the morning may interrupt your energetic flow or cause issues if you are already crunched for time. Do as much of the preparation for your morning workings the night before. You can make theses preparations a part of your nighttime routine. Preparations – like shower steamers – take more time, so always be sure to plan when you can.

Morning Revitalizer

This working is for those of you who don't mind mornings but still have an issue with grogginess when they wake. Morning brain fog can easily be lifted with this citrusy recipe for a shower steamer. To use a shower steamer, you place it on the floor of your shower and the water activates the baking soda to release the scent of the essential oils. To make it last longer, place it on the opposite side of the shower from your drain so the water hits it, but it isn't standing in water.

Shower steamers are like bath bombs, the main difference being the amount of moisture used when making them. Shower steamers are drier and therefore denser, making them take longer to dissolve in water, but they can still be used in the tub too.

For this recipe you will need:

- A mold for your steamers – generally these are square shaped about an inch thick, but you can choose any design you wish.

- 1/2 cup baking soda

- 1/4 cup citric acid

- A spray bottle filled with witch hazel

- 7 drops lemon essential oil

- 7 drops orange essential oil

- 7 drops tangerine essential oil

- Plastic gloves

Wearing plastic gloves, blend the baking soda and citric acid, ensuring it is mixed well. Add the drops of essential oils, spreading them out as much as you can over the dry ingredients. Blend extremely well, being sure to break up any clumps. Mist the mixture with a spray of the witch hazel and blend together again. When you are able to press the mixture into a shape and it stays, it is ready. If it does not stick yet, add another spray of witch hazel and mix again. Repeat until you reach the desired consistency. Pack the mixture into your mold and allow to sit overnight. Remove the steamer from your mold and either use it or store it in an airtight container.

As you prepare the steamer, instill it with your energy. It contains several distinct kinds of energy already from the ingredients, but you should add your energy as an additional ingredient. Visualize your energy charging this mixture with joy and happiness. You can add more energy to the process by adding music while you work. A couple of lit yellow and orange candles in your workspace help to instill your working with joy and energy.

While you blend your ingredients together, use this chant to build focus and direct your energy into what you are doing:

This song I sing,
To my work will bring,
Magic from my soul
Energy raised,
Focus sent,
Mixing in this bowl.

When you are ready to use the steamer, place it on the floor of your shower or pop it into the tub if you are taking a bath. As the water hits it and releases the scent into the air, close your eyes, take several deep breaths, and allow the scent and water both to wash over you. Visualize the citrus scent scrubbing away at any gray grogginess with bright yellow and orange colored energies.

As you visualize this happening, reach out to the deity of your choice, or to the universe and say:

Please help to take away that which clutters my mind,
Wash away what interferes with my ability to be at my best.

Bless me in your peace and light as I look to you for guidance on my path.

Let it scrub away the brain fog, which is then washed down the drain.

Refresh and Recharge

This working is for those who have a physically tough time getting moving in the morning. If you suffer from chronic pain or inflammation, this one is directed toward you. You can get your ingredients with a trip to the produce section of the grocery store, a farm stand, or your own herb garden for a bunch of fresh peppermint and rosemary.

To make this type of working easy in the future, you do need to do some prep work in your shower, but once it is done, you will be able to use it over and over for this and other workings. Place a plant hook in your shower ceiling so that when you hang your herbs from it, they will be hit by the water close to the shower head. Tie a ribbon or string to the hook, and on the other end attach a spring-activated clothespin. Make the ribbon or string long enough so that you can easily reach it and yet pin it up out of the way with the clothespin when not in use.

Prepare the herbs the day before by tying a string around the stems of the peppermint and rosemary, bundling them together. If you happen to a yellow or orange ribbon you can use, all the better to add in a little bit more focus and boost the energy. As you wrap the string or ribbon around the stems to bind them together, focus on your intent. When you use this bundle, you want to feel refreshed and recharged, ready for the day. You want pain to subside. You want positivity. Think about those things now and pour that intent into the plants as you wrap the string around their stems and tie it. Store this in the refrigerator until you are ready to use it.

When you are ready to shower, throw on a playlist that makes you feel energized. Take the bound peppermint and rosemary bundle and use the clothespin to snap it in place in front of the shower head before turning on the water. Scrunch the fresh leaves in your hands a few times and appreciate the feel of the coolness against your skin. As you scrunch the leaves, you release their essence and energies. Turn the water on and allow the water to pass over the leaves and to you, carrying the energies with it.

If you prefer to use a bath, prepare the herbs as mentioned. Scrunch the leaves under the running faucet as the tub fills. When you gave your desired water level, use the herb bundle to stir the water in a clockwise motion. Remember to send a healing intent into the water through your herb bundle.

Close your eyes and take several deep breaths, allowing the scent to fill your head and lungs. Take in its healing properties. Take in its power to refresh you allowing you to feel re-energized. Keep the herb bundle in place throughout your shower, or let it float in the tub with you. When you are finished, use the bundle to gently shake off the excess water over yourself. If you can, allow yourself to air dry naturally. You can reclip the peppermint and rosemary with the clothespin to allow it to dry out and to leave your bathroom smelling fresh.

Spiritual Cleansing

Remember, maintaining spiritual health is as important as maintaining your physical and emotional health, which means spiritual cleansing is as important as physical and emotional cleansing. You may feel you need spiritual cleansing for varied reasons. While a nightmare may leave you feeling spiritually vulnerable, you may also feel the need for spiritual cleansing due to the ingrained trigger of guilt. Whatever your reasons, they are your reasons and between you and your higher power or higher self. Because we need to take our spiritual health seriously, this working will be a ritual style to help convey its importance.

Set the scene with:

- A white candle in a fire safe container in a safe place in or near the shower or tub.

- A second fire safe container with a handle – this one should have either sand or salt in the bottom and a self-lighting charcoal tablet on top of the sand/salt. Ensure the bottom will not get too hot and scorch whatever it is set upon. This too, should have a safe place to sit in or near the shower or tun. A small cast iron cauldron would be perfect.

- A lighter

- A mix of frankincense and myrrh resins – as little or as much as you like. You can always start small and add more if you want to.

When you are undressed and ready, light the white candle and call to your deity, the universe, or your higher self by saying:

I call upon {insert name or title}
As I perform this sacred consecration.
Be with me now to guide my path.

Light the charcoal tablet in the fire safe container. (An open window is always a good idea when working with self lighting charcoal tablets.)

Once it is ready (has turned red or ashen), add a few pieces of the frankincense and myrrh resins to the charcoal tablet. They will start smoking immediately. Using the handle, move your cauldron or container all around the shower area, filling it as much as you can with the smoke and then placing it in a safe spot. Keeping the door or curtain closed will allow you keep more smoke in the area but be sure not to make it too smokey as to cause any breathing issues. Do not yet turn the water on, but instead, begin "bathing" yourself in the smoke. As you bathe in the smoke, say slowly (take your time as you allow the smoke to drift around you) either to yourself or aloud:

> *I stand in sacred smoke,*
> *Naked before the universe,*
> *My spirit and soul to be cleansed.*
> *I stand in sacred smoke,*
> *Naked with the universe,*
> *My spirit and soul at one with all.*
> *I stand in sacred smoke,*
> *Naked before the universe,*
> *My spirit and soul cleansed.*

When you are ready, turn on the water and visualize your spirit being rinsed clean as the smoke disperses. Finish by showering or bathing as normal.

Healing Waters

While this isn't guaranteed to heal all that ails you, it will help clear stuffy sinuses, congested lungs, a scratchy throat, and possibly a headache. These types of symptoms aren't what you want to deal with starting off your day, so if you feel an illness coming on, be sure to pick up a bunch of fresh eucalyptus to keep on hand.

Tie up the eucalyptus with twine to hang on the hook with the clip in your shower or place it so the water from the tub faucet will run over it. You can leave fresh eucalyptus in your shower for about three weeks, which should be plenty of time to clear your head or chest.

Eucalyptus has incredible healing energies, but we won't leave it up to just the plant. To prepare for this working, find a safe place for some green candles. (If there is no place i n your shower or tub where you can safely use candles, don't forget the tank on the toilet. This often a place where you can set up some candles in safety containers. Don't use taper, chimes, or spell-size candles. Instead use jars, tins, or votives in holders.) Add some waterfall music on a nearby device, and you are ready to begin.

Before entering the shower or tub, ensure the eucalyptus is hanging where it will get wet. Allow the shower to run as hot as it can for a few minutes to build up steam and release the scent from the eucalyptus. Be sure to turn the water cooler again before getting in! Inhale deeply through your nose several times while exhaling through your mouth. Switch your breathing pattern by inhaling through your mouth a couple of times while exhaling through your nose. This is a little bit more difficult to do, so be aware of the possibility of getting light headed. Return your breathing to normal.

See yourself feeling better, breathing easily, all signs of malaise are gone. Focus on this image as you breathe in and out, inhaling the healing scent and energies of the eucalyptus.

Finish your shower or bath as normal. After you get out again, turn the water as hot as you can to steam up the air with the eucalyptus one more time to get one last boost.

For morning work, before you leave the shower or tub, for the last few second turn the water cold for an invigorating splash.

While a shower of bath will not cure everything, it does give you the space and time for a reset to help keep you on the right path. One step at a time gets you where you need to be.

Bath Workings

Taking a bath at night is not only a relaxing, soothing way to wind down at the end of the day, but also a wonderful way to add more water magic to your day. These workings include bath salts, a meditation, and an affirmation.

Wash Away the Day Bath Salts

These bath salts will help you release what ails you after a long or tough day. While you are combining ingredients and blending them together, send peaceful, relaxing energy into what you are working with. Visualize something you find to be peaceful or use your energy color representation and send peaceful energy into your working. What can you add to your workings to make it stronger? You can light candles in corresponding colors. Working with relaxing music will help you to boost this energy.

For these bath salts you will need:

- 1 cup of any combination of bath salts: Epsom salts, sea salt, pink Himalayan salt

- 2 tablespoons dried lavender buds

- 2 tablespoons dried chamomile buds

- A bowl and spoon or spatula for mixing

- Any 8 – ounce jar with a lid

- Optional: colloidal oatmeal for baths

Combine all the ingredients in a bowl and mix until well combined, then transfer into a jar that has an airtight lid. Depending on how much you choose to use this mixture should last 2-4 baths.

Wash Away the Day Meditation

Using the bath salts above, prepare your bath with comfortably warm water. Add relaxing candles where (and if) it is safe to do so. For your audio pleasure, do a search for "waterfall music." This will give you plenty of options that include relaxing music with the natural sounds of waterfalls and moving water.

If you are comfortable with it, turn out the lights and use candlelight only. (If you cannot burn candles safely, try night lights, tap lights, or battery operated candles.) Submerge yourself in the tub and get comfortable. Allow yourself a few moments to appreciate the warmth of the water. Close your eyes and take several deep breaths, inhaling for a count of five, holding for a count of five, and exhaling for a count of five.

Listen to the music with the sounds of flowing water. Visualize yourself in a serene sitting where you can bathe in a private lagoon filled by a waterfall, It doesn't have to be a huge, grand waterfall; a small one, with the strength of a strong shower, is plenty. This area is for you, so make it what you want it to be. Add in any details you like or make it as vague as you like.

You are here to relax and wash away any stress from the day. This doesn't mean you are forgetting about any problems, only stripping away the stress any problems brought with them. We can learn to deal with our problems without letting stress get to us; we only have to learn how. Problems are seldom solved by stress alone. Once we realize we decide how we are going to react to problems, dealing with problems get easier. That isn't to say they go away, but we can learn how to handle and solve them while not letting them bring additional fallout along for the ride. Since we don't need stress to solve our problems, we can let it wash away.

Imagine you are washing away all stress or other negativity at the end of the day. Maybe you watch it roll off you as you float in your private lagoon. Maybe you watch it wash off like chunks of mud as you stand underneath the waterfall, water running all over you. Perhaps you visualize stress and negativity as a dingy color that washes from you and swirls away downstream. See yourself being cleansed of stress and refreshed. When the stress is gone, we can function and sleep better. Being sure not to take stress to bed with you isn't easy. It takes conscious effort of ridding both your mind and body of it first. Making these conscious efforts to put your own emotional well being first is self-care at its finest.

Wash Away the Day Affirmations

Adding in affirmations help tell yourself what you need. When your body and mind want to hold on to stress, tell it to stop and let go instead. This is part of how affirmations work – repeating something enough makes it come true for you. It's an incredible power that we have, and we need to make sure we are using it properly.

After you have washed the stress away with your meditation but before you leave the tub, use any of the following affirmations to back up your working. You may pull the plug and allow the water to drain away as you finish.

- My stress is washed away.

- I am in control of my reactions.

- What does not serve me washes away.

- I am cleansed and free from stress and negativity.

- I am refreshed, relaxed, and ready for bed.

When you are finished, have comfy clothes ready to wrap yourself in.

Medicate and Meditate Healing Bath Salts

Whether the medicine you use in your life is a pharmaceutical, cannabis, CBD, or the act of relaxing in the bath, you know what helps heal you and makes you feel better. This working is all about healing.

Use this tub time working to medicate however you need to and then follow up with the healing meditation and affirmation below.

For these bath salts you will need:

- 1 cup Epsom salts

- 1/2 tablespoon dried chamomile

- 1/2 tablespoon dried lavender

- 1/2 tablespoon dried peppermint

- 1/2 tablespoon dried rosemary

- A bowl and spoon or spatula for mixing

- Any 8 – ounce jar with an airtight lid

- Optional: colloidal oatmeal for baths

Combine all the ingredients in a bowl and mix until well combined, then transfer into a jar that has a lid. Depending on how much you choose to use, this mixture may only last one to two baths. (You may use it all at once or half a cup at a time.) Epsom salts are beneficial to healing aches and pains, but you do need to soak for at least twenty minutes.

Healing Meditation

Increase your healing energies by combining your healing bath with a healing meditation.

Adding green and/or blue candles in fire safe containers where you can, will add extra healing energies to your working.

Begin running the water for your bath. Hold the jar of salts in both of your hands and say either aloud or to yourself (directed toward your higher power): *Bless this salt and these herbs with your healing touch.*

Imagine what the energy of the blessing would feel like. Visualize it. Feel it. Honor it.

Slowly scatter the salt in a clockwise motion around your tub. As you scatter the salt, watch how it incorporates with and then dissolves into the water. The energies are combining. The herbs will float on top, the water steeping their essences out to blend with the salted water.

After you have added all the salts, use your hand to gently stir the water three times clockwise. If you have quartz or hematite stones (hematite will eventually rust in water, so do not repeatedly use the same stone), you can hold these in your hand as you stir and then drop them into the tub. Again, you are adding more healing energies with everything you bring to your working. While you stir, visualize all these different energies mixing; see each as a distinct color swirling together into a portal of healing. Step into this portal and get yourself into a comfortable position. Towels can be rolled to place behind the back of the neck if needed. Once you are comfortable, begin some deep breathing. Inhale and exhale, holding each for a count of four several times, then followed by holding for a count of five for several more.

Allow your body to relax. Water allows you to feel lighter; enough of it can make you feel weightless. Focus on this feeling. Allow yourself to float as much as you can, both physically and spiritually. See yourself floating in the healing portal of energies. Visualize the healing energies swirling around you in a clockwise motion, scrubbing pain out of you and into the water to later be washed down the drain. These energies regenerate and rejuvenate where needed. Out with the old, dull, painful energy. In with clean, fresh, pain-free energy.

Remember, Epsom salts need twenty minutes to work optimally, so you need to plan to stay in the tub at least that long. If you need to, warm up your water. When you are ready to leave the tub, pull the plug and stand while you visualize the pain swirling down the drain. Let it all go.

Healing Affirmations

Boost your healing energies by adding in affirmations.

These can be done before, during, or after your bath, and whenever you feel the need to boost your healing power.

- I work to heal myself.

- Strength surrounds me. It permeates me. It makes me healthy and strong.

- I am whole. I am complete.

- My body is strong. My spirit is strong. My body and spirit work to heal me.

- I release pain. I release illness. I release all that ails me.

Water magic is, by its very nature, cleansing. Remember to focus on washing away whatever negativities you must contend with, while enriching your spirit with positive energies instead.

Journal Exercise

What role has water magic previously played in your spiritual practice? Be sure to document your workings in a journal or your Book of Shadows with your thoughts, results, and any other valuable information.

Chapter 5
Love, Pray, Eat

Food is our most important source of energy, and one we must replenish daily to survive.

It is important to understand your relationship with food, evaluate if it is a healthy relationship, and if necessary, make adjustments where needed. A healthy relationship with food includes not overindulging, knowing and understanding what your food is and where it comes from. This knowledge changes your attitude, allowing you to achieve true gratefulness for what you have. It helps you to gain a new perspective and appreciation. Most importantly, your food is your main energy source. Be mindful of what kinds of energies you are consuming. Your body is your temple, don't fill it with trash.

Natural foods allow you to connect with the energies of the earth they came from. Highly processed foods do not contain these natural energies, instead they have been stripped of nutrients and often contain dangerous and poisonous chemicals which have had a profoundly horrible effect on American life which goes unnoticed by millions every day. We have become so unattached to our food; we seldom have any clue what it even is. We have forgotten it is our main source of fuel and not just another form of pleasure, resulting in poor choices and inefficient energy. Flower children know Mother Nature knows best.

Understanding what is in your food allows you to make a stronger connection with it. Preparing food yourself is the best way to ensure you know precisely what is in it. When you prepare your own food, you can also bless it as you work. Some religions have extremely strict codes dating back centuries for how they prepare and bless food. It is not a new idea, but one that often been pushed to the side in exchange for convenience and often lower prices. The prices are lower because the food is less real food.

Just a few decades ago, in my lifetime, the processed food market barely existed. Today, we are bombarded with bad choices, and even worse, bad choices disguised as good ones. It is imperative we each make safe, healthy food a priority, not only for ourselves, but for everyone. Go to farmers markets and buy local when you can. Grow your own when you can, and most importantly, share with others when you can. Community gardens need to become a prominent local feature in our landscapes. Renormalize gardens over lawns. Those who have available land for gardens, reach out to those who don't. Shared gardens with shared responsibilities and shared harvests help build healthier communities.

Preparing your own food has other fabulous benefits. The popularity of baking sourdough bread during the pandemic lockdown provided comfort, entertainment, sustenance, and a way to create something new in an environment which was ripe with heavy feelings of hear, suffering, and death. Sharing starter and baked loaves became a new way to build connections and community.

When preparing your food, focus and direct your energy and intention into your preparation as you would with any other working. The ingredients you use can support your intention and will contribute their own energy. The setting in which you create your recipes will also contribute to the energy you infuse into them.

Lighting colored candles, playing music, burning incense, or diffusing oils into the air, even dancing, are all ways to help build, focus, and direct your energy while preparing yourself a meal.

As you recite a blessing, hold your dominant (or power) hand over the food you are working with. Visualize the energy transferring from your and into your meal. When you are finished with a blessing, you will want some type of closing to tie it all up. Closings include "Amen," "So mote it be," "Blessed be" or even a simple "The end."

Music, incense, and candles during a meal help to set an ambience to emphasize your intention.

Journal Exercise

Evaluate your relationship with food. What does food mean to you? What healthy and unhealthy eating habits do you have? Observe your current food related practices. How connected/disconnected are you from your food, where it comes from and how it is prepared?

Salt and Pepper Protection Blessing

I love to use a bit of kitchen witchery in my practice, and there are many simple ways to do so. One of the easiest is the act of adding salt and pepper to a meal. Not only do these spices add a wee bit of flavor and pizazz, but they also add protection. Since they both have protective properties, you can focus your intentions on infusing a dish with protection for the person who eats the food.

Chant the following as you sprinkle salt and pepper into your recipes:

Salt of the earth,
Pepper from the vine.
Let us work together,
Protect what is mine.

Easy, to the point, and effective.

This should be just the beginning of learning the properties and correspondences of the herbs and spices you use. Having this knowledge gives you more control over what energies you direct into your food preparation.

Healing-Infused Food Blessing

It doesn't matter what type of food you are preparing; you can use this healing-infused working for anything. Whether it's a gourmet meal or pouring a cup of coffee, all that changes is how long you keep your working going.

To begin this working, I want you to shake your arms and hands in the air for a minute or two first. Really shake them. Feel the energy in them? Visualize the energy you feel as green. Whatever shade of green you want but be sure it is bright and vibrant. A shade of green that looks rich and healthy to you. Visualize the green energy transferring from your fingers to the machine, the cup, the spoon, the water, if there is one – a pod – everything you touch, infuse your healing energy into it. Let it travel a path from you to the final food or drink product you make. Once it reaches its destination, allow the energy to swirl, scatter, and dissipate, being absorbed by what you made.

Working with green candles lit and a healing scent such as eucalyptus, tea tree, lemon, or lavender in the air will help add to the energy you build and infuse into your meal.

Gratitude Food Blessing

Gratitude is an important aspect of any practice. When we work with manifestations or conduct spell work, we are asking to receive from the universe. There are many ways to give thanks for the blessings we have received and continue to receive. An uncomplicated way to practice gratitude is while preparing a meal, like some cultures pray and give thanks before eating.

A gratitude candle allows you to channel your intentions and is a great tool to enhance this practice. The candle can be any color that you associate with gratitude – green to represent the abundance in your life, pink for compassion and nurturing, light blue for peace and tranquility, purple as connection to a divine power, or white for unity and purity. Herbs associated with success and manifestation are great to use in gratitude workings, such as bay laurel, cinnamon, lemon balm, and Tulsi; also known as holy basil. These herbs can be burned as incense or used to dress your gratitude candle.

When you are ready to begin, clear you mind and set your intentions. Ensure that your space is cleansed and full of positive energies. Close your eyes and imagine a warm, soothing energy filling you from within, moving outward to fill your space and your food preparation items. Raise you hands, palms turned upward, and speak your intentions aloud. Express what you are grateful for using these words or choosing to speak from the heart:

I am grateful for the meal that will nourish me.

I am grateful for the love around me.
I am grateful for my abundant life.
I am grateful for all that I receive.

Release your hands as you release the energy outward and open your eyes. Continue to prepare your meal. Show your thanks by leaving a sample of the dish on your altar of placing some outside as an offering.

Energizing Food Blessing

This energized blessing will provide metaphysical fuel to your meal, nurturing not just your body but your spirit as well. Get high if you want to add in some far out psychedelic energy. Set your intention and prepare your space. Have your recipe and ingredients geared up in advance and get ready to move your body! Set the mood with uplifting citrus scents by diffusing some essential oils with an added drop of patchouli or slice up an orange and lay out the pieces. Open the blinds or curtains to let the sunshine in and light some candles.

Next, put on some music-anything that speaks to your soul and gets the blood pumping, whether it is an earthy drum jam, an electric beat, or your favorite hip hop hit. Choose something that empowers you, makes you feel strong, and aids you in tapping into your personal power.

As the music starts, close your eyes. Allow yourself to feel the beat and begin to sway to the sound of the music. As your body moves, imagine a bright yellow light building around you, warm and full of power. The light fills you while you dance. Direct this energy toward your ingredients and the kitchen tools that you will be using.

This next part may feel silly, but sound is an excellent tool for raising energy. Clap your hands together. Knock on the cabinet doors, drum on the countertops. Pick up a cooking pan and a spatula and bang them together. Laugh, sing, dance, and allow yourself to have fun with this practice. Fill your space with energy as you begin to follow your recipe.

Once your ingredients have all been added and your meal has been prepared, clap your hands loudly three times and declare:

I am energized!
My vibration is high.
Each bite fuels my body and mind.

Release the energy and serve your meal. Let the music continue to play as you eat. This is great for a social setting; allow yourself to laugh, rejoice, and feel the uplifting energy fuel you.

Positive Vibes Food Blessing

Add a groovy positive boost to any dish you prepare. Send positive vibes to yourself or to whoever else will be eating the food by setting up your workspace with yellow and orange candles along with music that makes you feel super groovy happy. If you are working with songs with lyrics, take the lyrics into consideration. For example, "Superstition" by Stevie Wonder is one of my favorite grooves, but the last thing I want to do is insert superstitious energies into my food, especially when serving others! Sound waves are energy waves, so be mindful of what energies you are sending. Keep it upbeat and positive.

Gather your ingredients together on a counter or table. Set the candles in a safe place close by and light them. As you light them, say:

> *I call upon the powers which be,*
> *To infuse my workings with positivity.*

Turn on your music, and as you prepare the meal, sing along with the song if there are lyrics. Visualize what positive vibrations look like to you. Maybe you see rainbows stretched out and riding through the air like waves. Perhaps positive vibes look like a giant purple smoke cloud after an awesome bong rip. Whatever you see as positive vibes is what counts. Send the energy you are visualizing into the food you are preparing. Watch as the energy soaks in and is absorbed by what you are making.

"Positive Vibes" is a hip playlist category to create. Dig it?

Welcome Morning

Whether you break your fast with a cup of coffee, a bowl of fruit, or a full Irish platter, take a moment before your first bite or sip to welcome the morning. If you can, go outside and face the rising sun. If you cannot go outside, gaze out an eastern window, or at the very least face the east. If you can see the sun, it may be easier to imagine the feeling the sunlight on your face as you close your eyes. Even if it is not visible, imagine this feeling, this warmth. The feeling of the start of a new day. Fresh. Ready.

If you are a hot coffee or tea drinker, holding your cup in your hands in front of your face adds to the warmth sensation -if there is no sun to warm your face, this may help enhance that part of your visualization. Be mindful of hot liquids and don't spill on yourself.

Take a few deep breaths as you enjoy the warmth on your skin and say either aloud or in your own mind:

Each day is a new beginning,
Each beginning a fresh new start,
Each day I welcome the morning.
Each morning, I open my heart.

Giving yourself these special moments throughout the day to connect fully with the present is another small act of self-care. Performing several small acts of self-care a day makes it easy to build these into good, supportive habits.

Meal Blessings

The act of blessing food goes back thousands of years and over hundreds of traditions. People the world over have seen the importance of blessing what goes into the body. When we can feel the connection between our body, food, and spirit, the act of blessing food adds a new importance. It becomes more of a necessity. Remember, your intention is what matters the most. Read the blessings and see how you want to use them and make a few adjustments for them to fit.

Breakfast Blessing

We often hear breakfast is the most important meal of the day. Your body has been in sleep mode, running on empty and hasn't had any fuel added to it for hours. It isn't easy to wake up, start your day, and be energized when your energy supply is wiped out. You can push a car with no gas, but only so far before you physically give out and can't go anymore. Your body is very much like a car out of gas when you first wake up. Skipping breakfast then ends up being counterproductive in the long run.

Taking the time for breakfast, even if it is a small one, helps set you up for a more positive, energetic, joyful day. Your body, including your mood, functions better when it is properly fueled.

Use this blessing for your breakfast to start your day off right.

> *This food is a blessing to my body.*
> *It restores my strength. It restores my energy.*
> *It provides sustenance for my survival.*
> *This food nourishes my body.*
> *It is a blessing upon my body,*
> *And I accept it with an open and grateful heart.*

How we start our day has a tremendous impact on your emotional well being. Starting it off with positivity gives you a wonderful base from which to build your day.

Lunch Blessing

I will be the first to admit, I do not usually eat on a regular schedule. This is something I have struggled with most of my life. It is difficult for me to remember to eat.

Our bodies need fuel. Starving them of this fuel has long-term side effects, including weight gain. Yes, not giving our bodies enough calories when needed causes our bodies to store more calories in case they are needed later. This lunch blessing also serves as a reminder of what our bodies need. When the body is happy, the mind has less to worry about, and we function more efficiently.

This lunch blessing makes for a happy body and mind.

Blessings upon this food.
Let it remind me food is sacred.
My health is sacred.
My body is sacred.
My mind is sacred.
What I take in becomes a part of me.
It feeds my health.
My body.
My mind.
Blessing upon this food.

You can use this blessing before you eat, or if you like, continually repeat it to yourself as you do eat. This makes for a powerful mindful moment you can accomplish while getting your lunch in at the same time, and it's a great break and reset before the rest of your day.

Dinner Blessing

While it is often said breakfast is the most important meal of the day, dinner is the one most people consistently eat. It is the last meal (late-night snacks not included). It is a moment to sit down, relax, and refuel. Sometimes, it is a celebration of having made it through the day. Let your dinner become a transition period for you. The hustle and bustle of the day is behind you. Even if you still things to do, take this time to downshift into slower gear. Allow your body to work with the natural rhythms of the world and begin the transition of winding down for the night. This is especially important for those who have a challenging time shutting down their mind to sleep. Instead of waiting until you are crawling into bed, begin the transition period at dinner-time and give yourself a head start.

Bless this food to nourish my body and restore my mind.
Bless this food to nourish my mind and restore my body.
Bless this food to replenish my energy as I ease into repose.
This day, not yet complete, has taken and given.
Help this food to restore my depleted energy.
Help this food to ground me as I recharge.
Bless this food and bless me.

This blessing reminds you to allow yourself the time to recuperate your energy. We live in a society that tells us to "go, go, go" all the time. Slowing down, recharging, and taking the rest we need is part of what gets us to – and keeps us at – our optimum selves.

Healing Blessing

Whether you suffer from chronic pain or a broken heart, blessing your food with curative energies helps you to release what ails you and work on healing your body and soul. This blessing works with your breathing as you inhale positive healing vitality and exhale negativity. Add green or blue candles to help build your healing energy.

Before you say your blessing, close your eyes and take three deep breaths. As you inhale, visualize positive energy flowing in through your nose. Let it lift away negative energy wherever it is stored inside of your body and then exhale it out loudly with a woosh through your mouth.

Bless this food to bring me healing grace.
Mend my [insert issue].

Mend my spirit.
Mend my soul.

Take another deep breath in and out slowly. Repeat the phrases above, followed by another deep inhalation and exhalation for a total of three times. Finish with your chosen closing. This blessing works with the power of your visualizations and relaxing your body to help the healing begin.

Remember, spells, blessings, and other workings don't have to be long to be powerful. When you are working with fewer words, it's easier to memorize them and use them repeatedly to build energy. Reputation builds considerable energy easily.

Energizing Blessing

When you need an extra boost of energy, bless your fuel to work at its most optimal efficiency. With this blessing, you will want to focus on visualizing pulling positive energy from the air around you and sending it through your power (or dominant) hand to your meal or drink.

Hold your nondominant hand out in front of you or to the side palm up. You will absorb the energy through this hand and then focus and direct it out through your dominant hand, which you will hold, palm down, over your meal or drink.

Yellow and/or orange candles boost the positive energy in the air, as will the scents of lemon, orange, or peppermint.

Visualize the energy cycle of pulling the energy from your atmosphere, through one hand, and out the other as you say:

From the air I claim the source,

Transform the energy and
Send it forth.
Boost my power,
Boost my might,
Energize this [food, drink, meal]
with vibrancy and light.

When you must read the words as you say them, it occupies some of your focus. Short and sweet can help you build your power by memorizing the words. Rhyming can also make memorization easier, allowing you to guide your focus more accurately.

Happiness Blessing

Finding a life that brings you true happiness is often considered the meaning of life. It's also often said anything worth having is worth working for. Life is not easy at times, and finding true happiness can be a long, hard trip with many bumps in the road. But the journey is worth it. We find great moments of bliss along the way, which can help sustain us and even revive us when needed. This blessing directs you to tap into previous moments of happiness to infuse your food with positivity.

When preparing to say this blessing, pull upon memories of joy. Picture them in your mind and recall the way you felt. Allow the feeling to come back to you. Draw on those feelings to create a new energy of cheerful enchantment and direct it into the meal you are blessing by visualizing it flowing from your dominant (or power) hand as you say:

Memories of happiness past,

I pull into the present.
The joy they brought me then,
I now use to augment
This meal before me,
Infused with sheer delight,
Take this conjured energy
To disperse in every bite.

Add candles of your favorite color to your meal to enhance the positive energy.

Building and maintaining a healthy relationship with food makes it easier to build and maintain other positive relationships. This starting point can help you to identify and either mend relationships or end ones that are not in your best interest. This new attitude and respect for food can help you discover new attitudes and respect in other areas of your life. Let it be the beginning of a chain reaction of healing.

I recommend reading *The Magick of Food: Rituals, Offerings & Why We Eat Together* by Gwion Raven (Llewellyn Publications 2020) for more information and insight.

Journal Exercise

Set up goals to build healthy habits and your connection with your food. For example:

- I will prepare 3 additional meals myself this week.

- I will research where my food comes from.

- I will spend 5 minutes in thankful meditation before eating.

Each week, evaluate and discuss your progress and results. Continue evaluating and evolving your practice.

Chapter 6
Bedtime Routines

Getting into a routine of winding down in the evening can help ensure the success of a good night's sleep. A good night's sleep is essential for us to be at the top of our game and for our bodies to be at their best. To function, we need rest. It is a simple fact. Yet, getting good sleep is often difficult for many people.

When we are children, our parents help us to establish a routine at night that is designed to help us shift from daytime extroverted energy to a calmer, introverted energy, which helps us drift off to sleep. As we get older, we often put these routines aside. The problem is, these kinds of routines work, yet we ignore them. They work because our bodies have a natural energy cycle called the circadian rhythm that works in conjunction with other natural energy cycles, especially the rise and fall of the sun. When we do not work with our body's natural energy cycle and instead work against it, we obviously aren't performing at an optimal level.

Reintroduce yourself to a nighttime routine. Shut off the TV, shut off the computer of tablet, put the phone down. Try some relaxing yoga. Prepare everything you need for the next day. Take a bath, read a book, read a book in the bath. Play relaxing music, use candle light, diffuse relaxing oils, or light incense. When it's time to go to bed, be relaxed and ready to go to sleep.

Everyone has a different schedule. My mornings don't usually start until 9:00 am. That is because I don't usually go to sleep until 2:00 am. I fought my body for a long time and would try to go to bed at 10:00 pm. All that would happen is I would lay there hour after hour after hour unable to sleep. I finally gave up and decided to listen to my body instead. If I can't sleep, I might as well be doing something constructive, and so now, most of my writing is done in the middle of the night after everyone else in the house has gone to bed and I can work uninterrupted. I do have a nighttime routine; I just start it later than most people start theirs.

Get It All Down

Take time as you are winding down for the night to prepare everything you need for the next day. Set alarms. Update your affirmation board. Spend time reading any upcoming meditations or workings that you need to start preparing for. Make lists of the things you need to do the next day; make lists of supplies you need. Take the time for any journal writings you need to do. Check in with your calendar. This is time for you to get everything prepared for yourself for later. Giving yourself this time to prepare and center not only your practice but also your life is another act of self-care people don't necessarily think about. It is a commitment to yourself to ensure your bases are covered and your work is done efficiently. Giving yourself prep time can help eliminate stress and anxiety in the future.

Journal Exercise

Spend a few days documenting your evening and how you wind down and get ready for bed. Next, review what you wrote and evaluate what actions you currently take to help yourself make this shift and any you take that are counterproductive to a good night's sleep. Do you have a routine or is every night more played by ear? What changes can you make to ensure you are getting the best rest possible? Begin making changes, one or two at a time for several days and then add in more if you need to. Always give yourself several days to begin building new habits before adding more changes on top of them. Making a few changes over a longer period is more successful than making a bunch of changes all at once.

Bedtime Meditations

These meditations can help you wind down your day, help you evaluate various aspects of your day, and of course, a body scan before bed is always an excellent idea. Depending on how your day went, different days will require different methods and meditations for decompressing. Choose which workings best meet your needs.

Evaluate the Day and File it Away

One of the reasons it can be so difficult to turn off your mind before bed is because you have had all these different things happen to you throughout the day, and your brain is looking for a way to compartmentalize it all. It needs to sort things out and store them away. Give it the chance to with this mediation

Begin by closing your eyes and taking a few deep breaths. When you think back over the day, what immediately stands out to you? Take a moment to think about and evaluate the situation. Was it a positive, negative, or neutral experience? Was this event something you will need to contend with again later, or is it over and done? Don't get caught up in the details of an event. Don't attempt to relive it. All you want to is look at it objectively and decide where you would like to store it for now. Take an inventory and pack it away. Visualize yourself sorting these events out and filing them where they belong. Trifles can tossed into a garbage can. Essential information can be locked in a safe. Issues from work can be left on top of a desk as you walk away. Once you pack away the things that come to you right away, scan back over the day, from the beginning to the present. Does anything else catch your attention? If not, that is fine. If there are still moments, conversations, or other issues that arise, continue asking yourself, "Where do I want to store this for now?" and then visualize yourself putting it there. When you are done sorting and storing, tell yourself they are put away for the night. They are not coming back out. Everything can wait until it is time for them to be dealt with. Until then, they are put on hold and need not bother you. Remember, the more you tell yourself something, the truer it becomes.

When everything is packed away, go about your bedtime routine as usual.

Bedtime Body Scan

Bedtime body scans are especially beneficial for people who suffer from chronic pain. If you want to add a scent to the air or play some music, set it up and get into bed, lying flat with your head on your pillow. You can cover up with your blankets if you want. Close your eyes and relax. Take several deep breaths Inhale for a count of five, hold for a count of five, and exhale for a count of five.

Begin with your toes, curling and uncurling them, stretching them out as far as possible. Flex and bend the foot a few times followed by rotating the ankles in both directions. Make a note of any pain you come across, recognize it, send it some healing energy and move on to the next body area. Tighten and relax your calf muscles. Bend your knees by putting your feet flat on your bed and sliding them closer to you. Let your knees fall first to one side and the the other. Bring them to the center again and straighten them back out. Tighten your core muscles and let them relax. Continue scanning for any issues as you go. Wiggle your fingers, stretch them out far apart and then close them down into a tight fist before relaxing Lift your shoulders toward your ears and release. Turn your head both left and right; raise your chin high into the air and then pull it in again close to your chest.

If you found any issues, use this knowledge to make sleep more comfortable by arranging pillows, bolsters, or blankets in a way that gives your more support where needed. If you don't find any issues – great! Your body is ready for a good night's sleep. Give it one.

Nighttime Mental Relaxation

Night comes and our bodies are ready to rest – but sometimes our minds miss the memo. This is a simple mindfulness meditation to help calm the restless thought that may keep you up at night. Begin this mediation when you are fully ready to go to sleep.

As you are lying down, whether on your back, side, stomach – whichever position is most comfortable for you – find a spot to hold your gaze for a few moments. This can be done in the dark as well, as you want to look at something that is not moving. A spot on the ceiling, a picture on the wall Avoid gazing at something that moves such as a turned on ceiling fan, or an analog clock. Once you choose something to gaze upon, take a slow, deep breath in. Exhale, gently blink your eyes. Inhale a second time, slowly blinking on the exhale. Repeat this process for ten breaths, leaving your eyes closed on the tenth exhale.

Now that your eyes are closed, notice what thoughts come up. Take this time to practice acknowledging and releasing each thought. Did your grocery list come up? Tell that thought, "Okay, I've acknowledged you, and now I release you until tomorrow." By actively letting go of each thought, you are emptying your mind of distractions. You may find that many thoughts come up during this time, and that is okay. Acknowledge each thought – it is there for a reason – and the release it; let it go.

This mindfulness practice may take time, and some nights may be easier than other. Building a continuous regular practice will help you develop the skills needed to truly relax for a restful sleep.

Let it Go Meditation

While the song "Let it Go" raged in popularity among children, the title is also a message many adults can benefit from. We often have a challenging time letting go. We hold on to an outdated image or ourselves. We hold on to unhealthy habits. We fold on to feelings we don't know how to deal with. We hold on too many things that are not good for us. Change isn't easy and it requires work. That work often starts with letting go. Use this mediation on tough days. The days when something bad happens and the feeling follows you around. While this meditation won't solve your problems for you, it will help you clear your head to be able to better deal with the issue at hand when you are ready. It will help you to let go of the negativity that makes it difficult to achieve a good, stress-free night of sleep.

You can do this meditation while either lying in bed or sitting somewhere comfortable before getting into bed.

Close your eyes and take several deep breaths. Focus on your breathing. Feel the air as it fills your lungs. Blow the air out through your mouth in as heavy a sigh as you can muster. Really let it go. Visualize you are expelling every bit of air in your lungs and then refilling them completely.

Wrap both of your arms around yourself in a tight hug and hold it while you continue to breathe in and out as deeply as you can. Focus only on your breath. Any thoughts that come up, blow them out when you exhale and think to yourself, "Let it go." Let them all go. Let all other thoughts go and focus only on your inhalations and exhalations. In and out. You will feel a change, a release that takes place. This release may be accompanied by tears. That is perfectly fine and even ideal. Crying is an incredible release for pent up tension and anxiety. If tears do fall, let them. Don't attempt to hold back; there is no need to. Let it all go.

When you are ready, let go of your self-hug. Take a few more breaths, allowing them to become shallower and go back to your normal rhythm with each cycle. Be at peace and go to sleep.

Bedtime Affirmations

Affirmations at bedtime help you unwind, relax, and get a good night's sleep. They help keep you in a positive frame of mind. Choose an affirmation from these that will serve you purpose for the night.

Winding Down

These affirmations help you switch gears and slow down at the end of the day.

- I am at peace. I am ready to rest.

- I am calm. I am serene. I am in harmony with the universe.

- I rest to begin again.

- I welcome the peace of the night. I welcome serene sleep.

- I am ready to reset myself with sleep.

- I deserve rest. I am designed for it.

- I am worthy of a restful night's sleep.

- I am thankful for the opportunities I received today.

- I look forward to tomorrow; I say goodnight to today.

- Each night I say goodbye to an old me and say hello to a new me.

I Am Enough

Use these affirmations to remind yourself you are precisely who you need to be. Life is a journey with many stops along the way.

- I am well. I am loved. I am whole.

- I am right where I need to be.

- I am resilient.

- I accept and love who I am.

- I believe in myself.

- I am a work in progress.

- I am me, and that is all I need to be.

- I am worthy.

- I am everything that I need.

- I have respect for myself, others, and nature.

Release

When you have a difficult day, it is important to release negative thoughts and energies before going to bed. Use one of these affirmations to help you let go when needed.

- I release what does not serve me.

- I release myself from expecting perfection.

- I releases myself from my own judgments.

- I let go of worry. I let go of self-doubt. I am okay. I am me.

- I am not the mistakes I have made.

- I forgive myself.

- Today does not determine tomorrow.

- I let go and let be.

- I release the stress of the day.

- I choose to rest at ease. Worries are set aside.

- I acknowledge my mistakes.

Acknowledging the Positive

Just as important as letting go of the negative is acknowledging the positive. Choose one of these affirmations when the situation fits.

- Today, I achieved remarkable things.

- Today, I tried my best.

- I am determined and capable.

- I find the silver lining.

- I am comfortable with myself.

- I trust myself.

- I am warm. I am safe. I am protected.

- I am proud of myself today.

- I am my priority. Peace is my priority.

Groovy Mystical

Projecting an ethereal or spiritual atmosphere before bed can help deepen your spirituality and your connection to deity or the universe, and it can assist in dream work. These affirmations can help you set the mood.

- I listen to my intuition.

- I dream of wonder and hope.

- I am mindful and present.

- I look forward to my dreams.

- I am love. I am peace. I am the universe.

- I surround myself with love.

- I deserve peace. I deserve rest. I deserve me.

- I grow each day.

- I am the light in my own life.

- I accept and love myself for who I am

Affirmations can be done while getting ready for bed, lying in bed, during an evening wind down yoga routine, or in any other way you want. What speaks to you? I like to do nighttime affirmations in front of my altar while sitting on a meditation cushion. I set a mirror up on my altar, light an appropriate candle, and recite my affirmations into the mirror. Looking yourself in the eyes as you them adds a whole other level of energy. It becomes more than an affirmation; it becomes a commitment to the self.

Bedtime Prayers

If you work with a higher power, you may want to say a prayer of thankfulness and appreciation at the end of the day and ask for protection through the night. Bedtime prayers do not belong to any one religion or pathway. You are welcome and able to speak with your higher power whenever you want to or feel a need to, no matter who your higher power is. Open and close your prayers however you prefer.

Protection Bedtime Prayer

This prayer is not only easy to learn but also a quick way to ask for protection and peace throughout the night, while putting any negative feelings left from the day aside.

As I lay me down to sleep
I ask my [lady/lord/deity] to keep me safe.
Grant me strength, grant me peace.
Any negativity, I release.
Fill my heart with love and grace,

Protect me in your sacred space.
Shelter me throughout the night,
and wake me with your morning light.

When you say this prayer, visualize your deity casting a protective bubble around you in which you are protected and safe.

Dreamwork Prayer

Use this prayer for inviting your deities or higher spirits to send you a lesson or message through the the dreamworld for dream workings. Remember, if you have a tough time memorizing, you can write your prayers down on cards to keep next to your bed for easy access.

Through the dark I rest my eyes
While my dreams help me to realize,
Messages sent through the night
Can help me find the path of right.
You know what I am ready for,
I trust you won't send any more
Bring me visions to help me grow,
Show me what I need to know.
In the morning, when I open my eyes,
Let me remember where my mind flies.

As with spells, intention is also a crucial factor when it comes to prayer. When you become more proficient in learning from your dreams and you are emotionally ready, this is an excellent prayer to use with shadow dream work, as you can use your intention to bring you what you need to heal. Dreams can be a safe place for uncovering distressing information. However, dreams can also be a scary place for uncovering distressing information. Using this prayer before dream works helps to set up a safe environment. You will learn more about shadow work in a later chapter.

Prayer for Healing

When we need healing in our lives, we need to learn to ask our higher power for assistance. Asking for help isn't always easy, and many people have been taught asking for help is a sign of weakness. It is not. It is a sign of knowing your own capabilities and limits. It is a sign of self-care. There is no shame in asking for help. The real shame is how people have been taught they need to be strong 100 percent of the time with no help from anyone. It is an unrealistic expectation designed to make people feel like failures. We have set ourselves and others up with impossible goals of perfection. We are now learning to do better. Asking for help is a sign of a healing individual.

As always, begin this prayer by addressing your higher power in a manner that is comfortable for you and then continue:

I call upon [name] to send me aid and healing, which I need.
Stand by me through my suffering,
Help me shoulder this load.

Take a moment here to use your own words to describe what burden you carry. Is it emotional? Physical? Describe your ailment. What do you need to heal? Take as much time as you want to express what healing you need. Don't worry about sounding "just right". Relax. Imagine you are having a conversation with a beloved, trusted friend. You are. When you are ready, continue:

I come to you, with reverence, honor, and love,
And ask for your aid.
Help me to heal.
Pick me up when I am down,
Hold me strong when I am weak.
Show me light in the darkness,
Share your strength when I call.
Share your compassion if I fall.

End your prayer in your normal manner.

The word "fall" in this prayer refers to the stumbles we make while in the process of healing – whether literally or figuratively. Healing comes with setbacks, as it isn't always a straightforward well-lit road. Sometimes the pathway to healing is dark with unexpected twists and turns. Falling is just another obstacle along life's journey and often comes with lessons we need to learn. Society teaches us to look at setbacks as negative, but often they lead to a different, better solution than what was originally planned. A turn in the road is neither a positive nor a negative. It is just a turn in the road, which temporarily leads us in a different direction than what we expected. These side roads are still a part of our overall journey of life. How we learn to adapt to them is evidence of growth and enlightenment.

Prayer of Gratitude and Thankfulness

One of the best ways to find yourself in a more positive state of mind is to accentuate the positive over the negative. Focusing on negative feelings gives them energy. This isn't to say we ignore them – not at all. We learn to process them, learn from them, and move on. But, if we focus too much on the negative, we risk allowing it to overshadow the positive. Taking our time to give a prayer of gratitude and thankfulness at the end of the day brings the focus to all that we have and are. Not only is it a wonderful spiritual practice to be mindful of and thankful for what you have, it also puts your mind in a happy, grateful state before going to sleep.

Open your prayer as normal and then continue:

> *As this day comes to an end*
> *I thank you for all you send.*
> *I am grateful for all I have,*
> *I am grateful for all I am.*
> *I have joy in my life,*
> *And as I go to sleep this night,*
> *I remind myself of all that is right.*

Take to list your blessings. What are the best parts of your life? What are you proud of? What brings a smile to your face? What was the best part of your day? After listing what comes to mind, close your prayer as normal.

Remember, it's not only about the big moments in life. Each day brings us some sort of positivity. Sometimes the positive might be difficult to find, but it is there. Finding the good and giving thanks for what you have is an effective way to calm the mind and put yourself into a better state before drifting off to sleep.

Journal Exercise

Begin creating your bedtime routine by implementing a couple changes at a time. Every 2 weeks evaluate how you are doing with your changes and add in new ones. Work on being consistent. What differences do you notice?

In the last few chapters, we have worked on analyzing our current patterns and setting up new daily routines that help incorporate more spirituality and positivity into our life. Throughout the rest of this book, we will cover spells, rituals, and other workings to help you through heavy times while boosting self-love and self-esteem.

Chapter 7
Workings for Self-Esteem

For years now, I have been hearing from Pagans, witches, and other people they suddenly feel like their eyes have been opened and they are seeing things differently. While some people call this being "woke," it truly is a type of enlightenment. When you feel a veil has been lifted from your eyes and you see things from a different point of view, you are experiencing a side effect of enlightenment.

With the emergence of The Great Awakening, many people are learning new truths about themselves. This truth often includes the idea we deserve more. We deserve better. We have settled. We have accepted. We have done what the establishment has told us to do, often without question, because "That's the way it's always been done."

Sometimes, we discover we have been wrong about things. Being wrong is okay. It means we have the opportunity to learn. Awakening to a new truth also means working through it.

Every generation has its progressive members who work to bring a better future for the inhabitants of the earth. It is no mistake nor coincidence the call to witchcraft was heard by millions of ears during 2020, a year which began with the worldwide pandemic and ended with the Great Conjunction. The events since then have shown our current systems are unsustainable. We know this is a sign of turmoil to come. We also know the phoenix rises from the ashes and a near brighter future is born.

We are realizing (finally!) on a broad scale, the idea of perfection is subjective. One size does not fit all. We do not have to fit into some generic mold. We are not all the same, nor do well aspire to be the same. We are unique individuals who need to celebrate our differences and learn from them instead of fearing and attempting to control them. We are all valid because of our individual beliefs and experiences, not in spite of them.

Issues with self-esteem can arise from a variety of causes. We will discuss later how shadow work can help you find causes when they unknown to you. It is important to remember magical work is always to be backed up with mundane work. Seek a therapist if you need one. Awakening isn't easy work.

The workings we do here are designed to help boost your overall self-esteem. Work through them whenever you need, as often as you need. You can do these before you begin or in conjunction with shadow work. Reclaim your power.

Primal Confidence Booster

Whether you find this working silly or deeply serious, either way, it works. You can use it when you need a seriously deep working, or you can use it when you feel like being on the freer lighter, fun side of life. Remember to set your intention ahead of time as to what type of experience you want. Let your inner pet out for a romp or your inner beast out for a hunt.

Your first step is to find music which works for you. Something that for you represents a primal, animalistic nature. (Personally, I love "Lion" by Saint Mesa for this practice.)

Next, find a safe private location – indoors, outdoors, day, night – whatever works best for you, though I do love to do this outside at night when no one will see me anyway.

You will need some way to play music, feel free to set the song to repeat or make a short playlist with a few different songs.

Go to your location, turn your music on, close your eyes (hence the need for a safe place) and listen. Focus only on the primal aspect of the music. Let it move you. There are no judgments here at all. Move however you want. The old saying, "Dance like no is watching"? No one is watching. Yourself included. Dance. Crawl. Stalk. Do whatever your instincts tell you to do. Let those primal instincts take control. Don't think about it; just let instinct take over. Move. Growl. Purr. What do you want to do?

When you let go and tap into primal energies, you can feel your self-confidence boost. Primal energies do not judge. They are a part of who we are at the most basic level. They are a part of an energy force that has existed since the beginning of time. They are accepting and filled with a positive charge. Primal energies focus on survival; they are filled with strength, which you can channel into a boost of confidence.

Letting go can be difficult; don't feel bad if you can't completely do it the first few times. It takes practice. As humans, we are trained to subdue our primal energies. This is a time for you to not only call upon them, but to also explore and use them. Once you can unlock the door that keeps those energies inaccessible, you are able to better understand them. When you access them, you'll know. There is no doubt. The difficulty is in getting there. The key is in your hands, but the correct usage means letting the walls crumble so you can reach the door.

Keep practicing until you succeed. Besides, practicing this fun; every time you practice, you will get closer to full success, and it helps in the activity department too, giving a natural boost of adrenaline and endorphins, which also boost confidence. Even if you cannot fully tap into the primal energies yet, you are still gaining experience in detecting energy shifts and confidence-boosting benefits from each of your attempts.

Getting high for this working makes it easier to break the barrier into the liminal space.

Journal Exercise

Write about your experience. What music did you use? What animal or creature did you invoke? Did you feel the instinctual primal energy shift take place? If so, describe what you felt. What do you remember?

Self-Acceptance Ritual

I remember when I was a child, I thought when I was a teenage, I would suddenly feel different. I would gain some sort of insight that would totally alter my personality and make me feel like a different person. When I was a teenager, I thought it would happen in my twenties. In my twenties, I thought it would be my thirties. Eventually, I realized the event I was waiting for wasn't some outside stimulus that would grant me sudden enlightenment. It would take place inside of me. A true turning inward and seeing myself through the eyes of others instead of my own. It wouldn't be instantaneous either. Turns out, it can take a whole lot of work to find out who you really are, particularly if you are recovering from trauma or are suffering trauma you have not yet realized.

What is important to remember is this: You are who you are. No matter what that is, you are worthy of love. You are capable of love. You are an important part of the universe. You exist for a purpose. Whether you know and comprehend your purpose or not, it is okay. You have one, and you will find it when you are ready.

No matter where you are on your journey, you are right where you are supposed to be when you are supposed to be there. Your journey is specific to you.

In this ritual, you will work on embracing who you are at this point in your life. This is a ritual you can do many times over. Every new lesson you learn, every new experience you have, combine to create slight changes in who you are, so every time you repeat the ritual, you will be a different person than the time before. Ideally, you should perform it on (or right around) the full moon. You can make this part of a monthly practice, with each ritual an acknowledgment of your growth from the previous one.

Set the scene with:

- A mirror

- White spell size candle

- Pink spell size candle

- Holders for both candles

- A lighter or matches

If you work with an altar, you may want to set your candles and mirror up on it. You will want to be able to sit either on the ground or in a chair and see clearly in the mirror. Place the unlit candles in between your seat and the mirror, with the white candle to the left and the pink candle to the right.

Seat yourself to look in the mirror, close your eyes, and take a few deep breaths to ground and center yourself. Put other thoughts aside. Focus your attention on yourself. Open your eyes.

Say:

> *By the light and the power of the full moon,*
> *I celebrate all that I am.*

Light the candles.

Gaze deeply into the mirror, into your own eyes, in between the two flames.

As you gaze, continue to chant, *"I accept who I am."* Find your ideal cadence, I usually prefer to chant more slowly in a whispered tone when it has been a month of rougher trials, tribulations, or revelations. Other months, I find myself in a more positive state of mind and at those times, a more jubilant, energetic chant is called for. Experiment to experience the different energies you can create. Continue your chant until your candles burn down or you feel you are ready to extinguish them. Some traditions teach snuffing out candles to keep the energy contained, while others believe in blowing out the candles to send the energy to the universe. I am of the second belief system, but you what feels natural to you. Simply be safe either way.

We all have work to do for ourselves. Anyone who tells you they don't, has the most of all. We never stop learning. We never stop growing. Not in this lifetime, nor the·next. Think of this ritual as a monthly stepping stone. Check in with yourself and celebrate who you are and where you are on your lifelong journey.

Journal Exercise

Expand or sum up your ritual with the journal prompt:

I am ...

What descriptors and qualities are you most proud of at this time in your life? How do you describe yourself? Who are you?

Forgiving Others

Always remember, giving forgiveness is not giving permission. It is not giving permission for someone to treat you in the same way again. It is not giving permission for the person to have access to your life if you don't want them to. Forgiveness does not mean you condone their actions. Forgiveness does not mean "it's okay" if it really is not okay. You can decide what terms are set when forgiving someone. You are allowed to forgive them and still tell them to get lost. You are allowed to forgive them and keep them in your life. You have the right to decide. You may also decide not to decide now what you want to do in the future, but know your heart is ready for forgiveness.

This exercise is a multipart working. In the first step, spend some time (think days, weeks, not minutes), writing down who you want to forgive and why. It is often easier to forgive those who have harmed us than it is to forgive our own selves, so you will start there. You also want to clear out of your life any unfinished business with others. This will allow you to devote more time and energy to yourself. This is something you may have to do every now and then – anytime there is a reason in your life to forgive someone else and move on. The first time you do this, however, expect to produce a longer list than subsequent workings. Take your time and use your words and feelings to get it all down on paper. What was the situation? What was the outcome? Is it fixable?

Write down everything you would like to say to the people involved. Giving forgiveness may involve people that are no longer here. Are there people who have passed away who you are working on forgiving? Getting your feelings out of your mind and heart down onto paper is a healing act. You can envision removing pain as you write. Each time you add something new to your list, another burden is lifted. When we do not give forgiveness, the offending action and offender still hold a power over us. When we release ourselves from this power, we feel lighter, relieved, and less burdened. We do not have to continue to suffer from the wrongs of others. We can forgive and move on. Again, forgiving and forgetting are two different things, and it is up to you on how you decide to proceed after forgiveness is given.

Once you have your list compete and are ready to move on, you can start the next part of this working.

Set the scene with:

- A large enough area outside where you can sit down and form a protective circle around yourself.

- A fireproof container large enough to burn the pages you have written. This may be a cauldron you burn in, a fire pit or bonfire, or even a charcoal grill. (Do not burn things inside of a gas grill.)

- A lighter

- 4 white candles

- Representations of earth, air, fire, and water placed in their respective elemental locations (east: air, south: fire, west: water, north: earth)

- As many lavender buds as you want to use

- Moon water (prepared ahead of time)

- A small trowel

- Dirt or salt (This will have a symbolic meaning so do not worry if you do not have a lot.)

- Representations of your deities if you wish to use them.

- Soft, soothing music

- You may want something such as a meditation cushion to sit on to ensure comfort while you work.

To begin, set the 4 white candles in the circle around you at the halfway points between each direction (southwest, southeast, northwest, northeast) allowing them to complete the circle around you.

You may place the lavender and your papers anywhere inside the circle.

Take a few moments to center and ground yourself. Relax. Take a few deep breaths and focus your attention on the task at hand.

Don't be afraid or embarrassed to show emotion. Forgiveness can trigger a variety of feelings. Working through, letting out, and then letting go of difficult emotions is exhausting both emotionally and physically. However, it helps the healing process move along.

Begin by facing east (unless your tradition states otherwise). Call upon the earthly energies of each direction and ask them to join with you:

I call upon the energies of the east.
May the power of air come to me and aid me in my quest.

Light the candle in the southeast before turning to face south.
I call upon the energies of the south.
May the power of fire come to me and aid me in my quest.

Light the candle in the southwest before turning to face west.
I call upon the energies of the west.
May the power of water come to me and aid me in my quest.

Light the candle in the northwest before turning to face north.
I call upon the energies of the north.
May the power of earth come to me and aid me in my quest.

Light the candle in the northeast and find yourself a comfortable location to sit in the circle.

Call upon your deity by saying:
I call upon [name] to guide me,
To walk with me and comfort me.

Take a few more deep breaths and relax before continuing with the following.
I call upon these energies and [name(s) of deities]
As I am ready to forgive and move on with my life.
I have felt anger, hurt, pain.
It is time for me to put those aside.
To return these negative energies to the universe to be cleansed, recycled,
converted into something new.
I release those who have hurt me from the pain they have caused.

I release any anger,
I release any hurt,
I release any pain.
It serves no purpose for me.
I ask the energies of the earth: ground me.
Air, release a cleansing breeze to wash the negative away.
Fire, I give to you these offerings of my pain.
Burn them away. Take them away.

Set your papers on fire and allow them to burn. As they burn, sprinkle bits of lavender on them so it burns with the paper. Visualize the negative going up in the smoke from the lavender. Watch it go – the lavender releasing its own energy to cleanse the negativity away. It is released by the fire to be reabsorbed into the universe, converted to neutral energy, stored away like a battery for later use. When they are done burning, continue,

Water, wash away and cleanse any negativity that remains.

Using a bit of the moon water, first bless yourself on the forehead to wash away and cleanse any negativity that remains there. Do the same with your heart next. Finally, pour some of the water on the ashes of the pages you burned. With each action you perform, visualize the water washing away any negativity that may remain. With this action, your forgiveness becomes complete.

Earth, ground the energy. Restore it to the universe.

Scatter either the dirt (use a trowel if needed) or the salt over the ashes. Visualize the energy being grounded, becoming neutral until it is called upon to act in another time, in another place. With this action, you release yourself from the pain. You have grounded the energy, taking away its negative power. Use this time to sink in and let any emotions out that you need to. If you want to cry, this is the time to do it. Let all the negative energy seep away into the ground underneath you. The earth knows what to do with it. Let her do her work. When you are ready to move on, say the following:

I forgive because I am strong, not out of weakness.
I forgive in order to release a burden which isn't mine.
I forgive to heal myself.
I forgive in order to love myself.

You may continue in a meditative state for as long as you would like. When you are ready to close, thank and release your higher power(s). *[Deity} Thank you for your guidance, for protecting me and surrounding me with your love.*

Turn to the east and say:
To the east and the energy of air,
I thank you for your cleansing breeze.
I thank you for your power and release you.

Blow out the candle at the southeast as you turn to face south. Say:
To the south and energy of fire,
I thank you for your cleansing flame.
I thank you for your power and release you.

Blow out the candle at the northwest as you turn your face to north and say:
To the north and energy of earth,
I thank you for your grounding dirt.
I thank you for your power and release you.

Blow out the candle at the northeast and say:

I have forgiven.

I am healed.

I am whole.

So mote it be.

After finishing this working, do some grounding by lying on the earth and allowing it to absorb your extra energy. Another favorite way of mine to ground that my group and I joke about frequently is eating cheese. A good hunk of cheese does wonders for grounding.

Journal Exercise

Expand or sum up your ritual with the journal prompt:

I feel...

Express the emotions you encountered preparing and conducting this working.

Self-Forgiveness Ritual

Sometime we do things we regret; to make a mistake is the most human thing that we do. Whether we receive forgiveness from others or not, it is important to look within and offer that forgiveness to yourself. Forgiving yourself is a major step in the inner healing process. As we forgive, we are relieved of a heaviness that have been holding us back. This relief allows us to step forward to a brighter future.

For this ritual, we will craft an herbal incense blend used for self-forgiveness. We will use garden sage for inner healing and to promote wisdom and longevity. Hyssop is used to cleanse, purify, and lighten our vibrations. Rosemary assists with memory and focus. Basil brings luck, softens tensions, and heals rifts. These herbs can be charged before your ritual by holding on to each one, closing your eyes, and focusing on the intentions mentioned here. Once charge, place the herbs in a small dish on your altar until they are needed in the ritual.

This ritual can be done either indoors with a potted plant or jar of dirt or outdoors where you can connect directly with the earth by using the soil in your yard.

Set the scene with:

- Paper and pen

- Access to soil (outdoors, a potted plant, or a jar of dirt)

- Garden shovel or trowel

- Cauldron or fireproof dish

- Charcoal tablet

- Lighter or matches

- 1 teaspoon dried garden sage

- 1 teaspoon dried hyssop

- 1 teaspoon dried rosemary

- 1 teaspoon dried basil

- A small dish (to hold the herbs listed above)

Before beginning this ritual, take time to center yourself. Self-forgiveness can be an emotional exercise, so it is best to be prepared in advance and take some extra deep breaths. When you are ready, activate the charcoal tablet by lighting it until it sparks and ignites. Using your pen and paper and write the following:

I forgive myself for...

Finish the sentence; be as detailed as possible. It is important to be completely honest and authentic as you write. Take note of how these words make you feel but release any judgment you may be experiencing. Admitting to all your wrongdoings is key to truly moving forward. Take ownership of your actions. As you write, reflect on how the situation made you feel and what thoughts went through your head at that time.

Once you have finished writing, fold the piece of paper toward you three times and then recite:

I have made mistakes.
I take ownership of my actions.
I deserve forgiveness.
I forgive myself for the wrong that I have done.

Now, fold the paper away from you (3 times if you can). Afterward, recite the following:

I release this burden so that I may move forward.

Set the paper down in the center of your altar. The herbs listed in the ingredients will be used now as incense. Carefully add the herbs to the charcoal tablet – this can be done one at a time or mixed in the bowl and added all at once, whichever you prefer. As the herbal incense burns, take your self-forgiveness note and weave it in and out of the smoke, returning your focus to your intentions of forgiving yourself.

Next, it is time to bury the note. If indoors, a potted plant or jar of soil or dirt will do. If outdoors, you can use the dirt in your yard. Prepare your jar, planter, of dig a hole in the earth. Place the note inside and bury it beneath the soil. Press the soil down on top and repeat the following one last time:

I forgive myself for the wrong that I have done.
I release this burden so that I may move forward.

To finish this ritual, close your eyes. Wrap your arms around yourself in a tight embrace and bow your head slightly downward, Picture a healing, light energy filling you from within, washing away your burden and enveloping you in warmth. Take as much time here as you need, honoring yourself and sending love within.

When you feel ready, release your embrace, and take a few deep, cleansing breaths. Allow the herbal incense to burn out on its own fully. (You can leave it outside if you need to if it is in a safe place and will not be disturbed.) Come back to the cauldron of fireproof container after the herbs and charcoal have burnt out and the container is cooled. You can release the ash to the earth or wash it away – whatever feels best for your practice.

At this point, it is time to move forward. After completing this ritual, you cannot dwell on the past. It is time to continue living your life.

Journal Exercise

Expand your ritual with the journal prompt?

I am ready for ...

What do you look forward to in your future?

I Am the Only Me

You are a unique, awesome, totally wonderful, and delightful human being. There is no one else out there in the world just like you. There is no one else who has lived your life, has had your experiences, learned your lessons, or felt your emotions. No one else has touched the lives of the people you have in the ways you have. You and only you. In this world of billions of people, no one else is just like you. That makes you incredibly special. Sometimes you need to remind yourself of this fact.

In this ritual, you will be celebrating all the things that make you, you. Spend time planning this out. This shouldn't be rushed. Collect items, pictures, words printed out or cut from magazines, souvenirs, and other keepsakes or mementos that have significant meaning for you – things that are associated with who you are as a person. All these items should be used to decorate your altar. If you need to use a different location than normal for your altar, that's okay; you will be able to take it down afterward. If you need to use the dining room table, then use the dining room table. Be sure to include the other items you would normally use on your altar such as deity statues and elemental representations. Give this deep consideration. This is a shrine to yourself. How can you best represent the parts of yourself you want to celebrate? What traits and qualities do you want to express about yourself?

Add candles to your altar. Choose colors that speak to you or hold special significance. Check out candles in different shapes and figures too. Madame Pamita's Parlour of Wonders has the most incredible variety of beeswax figural candles, from apples to owls in their online store.

Make this altar as much of a representation of yourself as you can. This is your time to celebrate everything that makes you the special individual you are. Spending the time to contemplate and evaluate the representations you want to include gives you an opportunity to compile a checklist of who you feel you are. Top off your altar by honoring yourself with your favorite incense or diffused oil if you wish. Enrich your atmosphere with a playlist of songs that have meaning to you – a soundtrack of who you are.

When your altar is prepared and you are ready to perform your ritual, dress in an outfit that has significance to you. It can be as serious, casual, or flamboyant as you want. This is all for you!

It can be difficult to focus your attention so deeply on yourself. You may feel like you do not deserve the attention, but you do. If you feel this way, this is something you should address in your shadow work. For now, however, do your best to soak in your own limelight.

If you are using incense and candles, light them.

Take a moment to center yourself and then say:

Today, I celebrate a wonderful person.
A person who has seen good times and bad,
Happy times and sad.
A person who has loved, a person who has lost.
A person who is healing and who is finding [themself/herself/himself].
I am the only me. There is no one else like me.

Look over your altar at all the items you collected. Meditate for as long as you want on their significance to you. How do they represent you? What are your favorite parts of yourself? What do you like about yourself? These are the feelings you want to hold on to. These are the things that make you who you are. These are things that make you unique. If you want to, write the answers to these questions in your journal. Do not let your mind wander to who you want to be; you are celebrating who you are right now in this moment of life. It has taken a long time to get where you are. You have overcome obstacles in your way. Appreciate the path you have traveled for where it has brought you so far.

When you are ready to continue, say:

I am unique. I am my own person. There is no one else like me.
I accept, love, and honor the person I have become.
While my journey continues before me,
I celebrate the person I am now. Today.
Right here, right now,
I love and celebrate me.

Finish your ritual when you are ready by extinguishing your candles. Spend time after this ritual performing self-care that you enjoy – soak in the tub, give yourself a massage, enjoy a favorite drink or meal. Reward yourself with an extra dose of love and appreciation.

Journal Exercise

Expand your ritual with the journal prompt:

I am unique because ...

Make a list of the things which make you, you.

Affirmations to Light Up Your Life

Positivity breeds positivity. Send out what you want to attract back. Fake it 'til you make it. All pieces of advice that, honestly, are quite similar. We use positive affirmations to help put us in a positive frame of mind when we aren't in one. Let's be clear here: we don't think about feeling better when we are already happy. We look to feel better about ourselves and the world around us, when we don't feel great. There is a lot pain and misery and suffering in the world. It can be downright cruel at times. But we don't give up. We don't give in. We trudge through and carry on. We do so because even though there is pain, misery, suffering, and cruelty in the world, there is also love. There is joy. There is happiness and exhilaration. There is pleasure, mystery, and adventure. Life is much more than the negative things we encounter. Unfortunately, we live in a society driven by accentuating the negative. Advertisers tell us everything wrong with us to sell their products to fix our problems. The news, though informative, seldom has "good" news. We are bombarded with negativity daily. It can rub off, but we can protect ourselves and even fight back.

These affirmations are to help you feel better about your life and the world around you, especially when you do not feel at peace. Those moments are when you need to capture and harness positivity the most.

While affirmations can be performed anywhere and anytime, you can also take the time and effort to make your session more significant.

Sometimes I take a meditation pillow into my labyrinth or out into the woods to do affirmation workings there. I particularly love to do this at night in the dark with incense and candlelight. I can't help but feel a bit more magical doing my workings out in the woods in the middle of the night.

What makes you feel magical? You don't have to be doing a full spell or ritual to bring that magical feeling into your workings; in fact, you probably want to be working toward bringing that magical feeling into everything you do. You can make your affirmation workings as casual or as formal as you desire and mix it up as often as you want. You may only want to say your affirmations a couple of times, or you may want to chant them in trance. Do what you need.

I'm All That

Whether you are a bit on the downside or looking for a boost before a job interview, work your magic to boost your confidence with one (or more) of these affirmations:

- I am strong. I am confident, I am my best. I am strong, I am confident, I am blessed.

- I am intelligent. I am capable. I am confident.

- I draw in confidence. I release all doubt.

- Determination, poise, and spirit. I call all in and do not fear them.

- I pull the energy from around me, I let it in. Boldness surrounds me. (You can substitute "boldness" with whatever word works best for you: confidence, tenacity, courage, etc.)

Turn on the Glow

You are a being of light and energy. You radiate this light and energy to others all around you. When you feel your light is dimming, try these affirmations to recharge and brighten your glow.

- I am stardust. I am energy. I am the brightest light.

- Sunlight and moonbeams, moonlight, and sunbeams. Stimulate my glow. (Visualize working with the light from both the sun and moon.)

- I am a part of the light which shines upon the world.

- Brighten my way, brighten my day.

- I kindle the fire within me, flames of illumination to light the world around me.

To add in energy conversion while performing these affirmations, sit or stand in a comfortable position. It may help your visualization process to close your eyes. Hold your hands in a comfortable position with your palms facing any direction away from you. You are going to draw the energy from around you through your palms. As you repeat your affirmation, visualize collecting energy from the environment around you. Pull the energy into you through your palms. Feel it enter and travel through your body. Feel it combine with the vibrations of your voice as you say the words. Charge the energy with the words you speak as you release them both into the universe.

Let the Light Shine in Meditation

The combination of this meditation with these bath salts is to help you accept your own self-love without guilt. Many of us, particularly females, were taught self-care was selfish. We were not taught to take time for us. We were taught our role was to please others. Not ourselves. It is a substantial change for people when they learn that self-care is not only okay but also a good, healthy habit. Prepare these bath salts ahead of time so they are ready when you are.

Let the Light Shine in Self-Love Bath Salts.

For these bath salts you will need:

- 1 cup of any combination of bath salts: Epsom salt, sea salt, pink Himalayan salt

- 1/2 tablespoon dried lemon balm

- 1/2 tablespoon dried jasmine flowers

- 1/2 tablespoon dried thyme

- 1/2 tablespoon dried red or pink rose buds or petals

- A bowl and spoon or spatula for mixing

- Any 8 ounce jar with a lid

- Optional: colloidal oatmeal for baths

Combine all the ingredients in a bowl and mix until well combined, then transfer into a jar that has a lid. Depending on how you choose to use, this mixture should last 2-4 baths.

As you combine the ingredients together, remember to add your energy to those you are working with. What song makes you feel good about yourself? Play it or sing it while you are prepping. Pink candles represent compassionate love. Add some of their energy by burning one while you work and while you use the salts.

Let the Light Shine Meditation

This meditation is all about opening yourself up to self-love. It is quite easy to shut off from loving ourselves and treating ourselves with the respect and compassion we deserve. It is time to throw open the blinds and crack a window to let the light shine in on yourself. With this meditation you will use a closed window as a metaphor for being closed off to self-love. Opening the window in this meditation will allow you to open yourself up to let self-love in.

Sit or lie down comfortable in your self-love bath and begin this practice by closing your eyes. Picture yourself in a room inside a house, where the windows are covered with old, dark curtains. This could be someplace familiar and comforting to you, or a new place you create with your imagination. Look around, notice the details. What is it about this room that is comforting to you? How do you feel when you look around; what feelings, thoughts, or memories come up? These are things you may want to make a mental note of to reflect on later; for now, release these thoughts and turn to the windowed area.

How many windows do you see? What do the curtains look like to you? What material are they made of? What color? How do you feel when you see them? One by one, go to each window and fling open the curtains. What does the window look like to you? Wipe away any dust or debris and push the window open. Allow the sun to shine in, brightening and warming the room and brightening and warming you. Notice how you feel as you open each window. Imagine a warm breeze blowing through the window, cleansing the room around you. Feel the fresh air on your skin. Continue this pattern until all the windows are open, and the room is filled with bright warm light. Feel the warmth on your skin and take several deep breaths inhaling this new warm, fresh energy.

When you are ready to return to the present, keep your eyes closed to end this working with some self-love breathing. As you take a few slow, deep breaths, wrap your arms around your body in a warm embrace. With each inhalation, focus on filling yourself with compassion and kindness, releasing any negativity with the exhalation. Take as much time as you need here. Breathe in compassion and exhale any self-judgment. Breathe in kindness and exhale self-doubt. Breathe in self-love and exhale, releasing any last heaviness you may feel within.

Open your eyes when you are done. After completing this practice, it is important to spend some time writing about the experience in a journal. Revise the thoughts, feelings, and memories that came up during the meditation. Reflect on what you were feeling and why these things came up. What do they have to do with self-love? What can you learn from this experience? Continue writing as much as you need to without overthinking it – letting the words flow freely allows you to tap into your intuition and any hidden feelings. This is important for healing and moving forward with an open heart.

After this exercise, it is important to remember that self-love is an ongoing practice. This is not something that you do once and move on. You may repeat this meditation as often as you need to, or even just return to self-love breathing. Self-love practices should be a part of our weekly and even daily routines. Remember, you deserve to love yourself.

Courage Meditation

Changes and fear of the unknown are frightening. Courage is the ability to do something which frightens you. Courage therefore doesn't mean you do something without fear – it means you do it despite the fear. These bath salts combined with this meditation work together to help you set your fear aside and let your gumption shine through.

Courage Bath Salts

For these bath salts you will need:

- 1 cup of any combination of bath salts: Epsom salts, sea salt, pink Himalayan salt

- 1/2 tablespoon dried borage

- 1/2 tablespoon dried fennel

- 1/2 tablespoon dried St. John's Wort

- A bowl and spoon or spatula for mixing

- An 8 ounce jar with lid

- Optional: colloidal oatmeal for baths

Combine all the ingredients in a bowl and mix until well combined, then transfer into a jar that has a lid. Depending on how much you choose to use, this mixture should last 2 – 4 baths.

Courage Meditation

Prepare your tub and set your atmosphere. Use black candles to absorb your fears and red candles to boost your courage. Include music that emanates the feeling of power. Add your salts to your water, climb in, and take a few moments to relax with some deep breathing as you let the water warm you muscles.

Close your eyes. Take time to mentally define and describe what your fear is. Think as if you were describing it to a trusted confidant. Break it down as much as you can in your own mind. What is the realistic worst-case scenario if your fear materialized? This is a big step – thinking about and analyzing the worst-case scenario. However, answering "What if?" questions allow both our mind and body to experience and practice triggers while in a safe environment. Go ahead and think to yourself, what if your fear materialized, what is the worst that can happen? Give yourself time to think about and, most importantly, accept the answers you produce. You may have physical reactions – anxiety, nausea, tears – to some of the responses you produce. That is okay and expected. It's why we meditate on these things before we do them. We are practicing and allowing our bodies and minds an opportunity to adjust to a change at a slower pace to encourage and promote healing along the way.

Allow yourself to feel and process any negative reactions you have relating to this fear while you are in this safe, warm place. Visualize your fear as a colored energy and watch as it flows from your body and into the water around you. Instead of changing the color of the water, you see it stream like ink as it snakes toward the drain to congregate and hover, trickles slipping down the pipe. Take deeper breaths if needed to let yourself relax. Calm yourself again if necessary.

Exploring worst case scenarios gives us a great deal of knowledge to work with. When we know different possible outcomes, we can acquire tools or information to minimize unwanted results and boost the likelihood of positive ones instead.

Think about the information you have acquired. You may see something right away that lessens your fear and boosts your courage. If not, that is perfectly fine. You have given yourself material to work with later.

When you are ready, focus your attention to the drain. Your inky fear is balled up, floating there. Go ahead and pull the plug. Let the fear be sucked right down in a giant gulp.

Exploring your feelings about a situation before it happens lets you know what you are up against. It gives you the opportunity to arm yourself with tools and information to minimize the chances of a worst case scenario happening. Fear is a part of what makes courage possible. You understand the risks and proceed anyway.

Journal Exercise

What fears are you dealing with? What are the worst case scenario outcomes? What are the best case scenario outcomes? What aspects of your fears are out of your control? What aspects of your fears are under your control? Breaking your fears down into these smaller bite size pieces makes them easier to digest.

Having good self-esteem isn't about liking how you look. It is about accepting who you are as a person. It is realizing and recognizing the value of your self-worth. It is doing the arduous work to help heal yourself from past traumas. It is transforming yourself to be the person you want to be.

Chapter 8
Magic for Coping

Sadly, when my generation was younger, we were taught coping was far more about denial than it was about healing. We were told what didn't kill you made you stronger. We were told out of sight, out of mind. We were told if you don't talk about things, they would go away. We were not taught how to cope. We were taught how to ignore and were told that's what coping was. There may have been a few families where this was not the norm, but I assure you, for most it was. The idea of coping is different now from what it once was.

Today, instead of silence and denial, coping includes the key components of acceptance and healing. The whole idea of mental health is still relatively new, and it is ever evolving. If you read about mental health history, you will find it has traveled a very rocky road at times. Lobotomies and institutionalizations were once considered routine mental health treatment. We've come a long way. We are finally demanding the care and well being for the individual more than ever before, and it is about time.

In this section, we will begin with coping with loss and loneliness and then work on how to rediscover yourself as a part of your healing process.

Spell for Coping with Loss

For many, a proper goodbye isn't always possible. When this happens, no matter what the circumstances of loss are, it lacks closure. The heart, brain, and soul often need this closure to be able to say goodbye and address the issue of grief. Without the goodbye, there is a sort of limbo where the finality of the situation feels impossible to accept.

Even when there is a chance for a goodbye, it may not have met your needs for closure. It somehow felt incomplete. There may have been more you needed to say but couldn't. With this spell, you can take the time to express the things you wish you had the chance to say to your lost loved one. Find a comfortable place where you will not be interrupted and allow yourself to take as much time as you need.

Set the scene with:

- A white candle

- A fireproof container

- Dried rosemary

- Dried lavender

- Pen and paper

- Comfortable seat

- Optional: A photo or token in remembrance of the one you lost

- Optional: an envelope to "mail" your letter in

Allow yourself to sit comfortable and begin by lighting the white candle. Take some time to remember your lost loved one. Look through pictures, touch the tokens you have with you. Picture them in your mind. Imagine they are sitting next to you and think about the things you wish you could say to them. Then, begin to write. Using as many pages as you like, write a letter to your loved one. Tell them how much they mean to you, reminisce with your favorite memories. Tell them about your life today, share happy moments with them. Loss may also trigger feelings of anger. That is okay. Don't hold back any emotions; take this time to fully express yourself.

When you are ready, end your letter and sign your name. Sprinkle the letter with your herbs – rosemary for clarity, remembrance, and cleansing, and lavender for peace, harmony, and healing. Fold the letter, taking care to avoid spilling the herbs, and, if you choose, place it inside of an envelope. Light a corner of the letter with the flame from the white candle, then carefully place it into the fireproof container.

As the letter burns, take as much time as you need to ground yourself. Perhaps enjoy a mug of your favorite warm beverage. Once the letter has burned, you may scatter the ashes outside in the wind, releasing your words to the universe.

Coping with Loss Meditation

Address your grief through this meditation which can be as short or as long as you choose – it is truly up to you. As always, read the meditation in advance to prepare. In this mediation, you will speak to a loved one that you have lost, so it may be beneficial to prepare a script, letter, or outline before sitting down. When you are ready, find a comfortable seat, play quiet music in the background, and close your eyes.

As you close your eyes, you are transported to a garden. See it in your mind's eye. Feel the wind blow through your hair, the sun shining on your skin. Smell the flowers and listen to the birds sing. There is a pond in the distance where you see the reflection of the sun. This is a peaceful place. Know that you are safe here. There is no judgment, only peace.

Ahead of you, there is a picnic. Your loved ones are there waiting for you. They are laughing, smiling, talking amongst themselves as they bask in the sunshine and enjoy their favorite foods and beverages, When you are ready, go to them. Join the picnic.

Take this time to truly focus on whatever loved ones you wish to see. Enjoy the time with those that you have lost. Tell them the messages that you wish they would hear. Share stories of your life and hear their words one last time.

When you are ready, it is time to stand up and leave the garden. Say your goodbyes and know that they are always with you, watching over you. They are never truly gone, and they will never be forgotten. Honor the past but do not let it hold you back from moving forward into the future. Life goes on, and it is time to return to live your life.

After you leave the garden and open your eyes, allow yourself the time you need to return to the present. Hold space for yourself. It may be beneficial to journal about your experience.

Coping with Loss Affirmations

Affirmations to help you cope with loss can be added to your daily routine or used whenever else they are needed. Choose whichever works best for you.

- I accept loss is out of my control.

- I accept grief has changed who I am.

- I am taking my time to grieve.

- Grief is healing. I am healing.

- The pain I feel in my heart will heal.

- To feel loss means I loved, and love is the greatest gift of all.

- I am never alone in my grief. I am loved and supported.

- Grief is temporary. Love is forever.

- I am grateful for the time we were given.

- A soul is never lost. Only energy transformed until we meet again.

We experience different losses in our life – from death to losing a job, home, or friend. All are types of losses, and each will require their own unique journey of healing. The overall theme of loss, however, is universal.

Coping with Loss Prayer

Speaking with your deities, guides, your higher self, or the universe helps you to process feelings related to loss and for many is an integral part of the healing process. Sharing the pain of your loss helps to make the load a little lighter. Sometimes, it is easier to say things in a private prayer than it is to another human. Learning to say what you need to through prayer may help you to say things you need or want to say to other people in your life. Begin your prayer as you normally would depending on your tradition and who you work with. Then continue with the following:

> *I reach out, to ease my pain.*
> *I reach out for comfort in my time of need.*
> *I reach out for strength.*
> *I feel loss. I feel pain. I feel grief.*
> *Help me to process through these emotions.*
> *Help me to heal*

Take a moment to speak openly about your loss. Say whatever it is you need to get off your chest. We all have a multitude of feelings we encounter while experiencing loss. This can include anger. If you are mad, say so. Your anger is a legitimate feeling that can be safely expressed. When you are ready, continue:

> *I know I will heal when the time comes.*
> *I know I will carry on.*
> *But now, I honor the loss,*
> *I feel the pain.*
> *I work through my grief.*
> *Help me to process these emotions,*
> *Help me to heal.*

Close your prayers as normal. You may feel the need to journal after this prayer or to curl up in a blanket. Both options are equally valid.

Journal Exercise

Loss comes in many varieties. We lose people to death, relationship break-ups, both within and beyond our control.

We lose pets, homes, jobs, career promotions, and plenty of other things. All these losses result in some level of grief – even when the grief goes unrecognized or unexpressed. We bury it, cover it up. *What I can't see, can't hurt me.* Recognizing your grief is the first step in the recovery process.

What losses have you hidden? Shine the light on them.

Nightmare Sachet

Grief can utterly destabilize our entire lives. When we grieve, that emotional pain has a physical effect on our bodies in addition to our mental health. It is common for grief to trigger nightmares and restless nights. Sleep is important for our body, mind, and spirit to rest, recuperate, and heal. This sachet is crafted with simple yet powerful ingredients that help comfort and provide peace on those restless nights. Once the intentions are set to work, the sachet should be kept under your pillow as you sleep. Let this working relieve your nighttime tension and allow you the rest you need.

For this sachet you will need:

- A small drawstring pouch, preferably white but black would work too

- Dried garden sage

- Dried marjoram

- Dried lavender

- Dried chamomile

- Rose quartz

When you are ready, call upon any guides, deities, or spirits that you work with, or invoke your higher self. You may invite your guides to bless each ingredient as you focus on your intentions of peace, comfort and blocking nightmares.

Take the sage into the palm of your hand and call upon its intended purpose:

I bless this sage to cleanse my dreams and purify my spirit.
Help me build emotional strength and heal my grief.

Close your eyes and imagine a bright white light enveloping the sage as it is blessed and place it into the sachet. Take the marjoram next:

I bless this marjoram to cleanse my mind and bring happiness.
Help me relieve my grief and find joy again.

Allow the bright white light to bless the marjoram and add it to the sachet. Move on the lavender:

I bless this lavender to encourage mental wellness and harmony.
Help me find peace and restful sleep.

Once the bright white light blesses the lavender, add it to the sachet. Prepare the chamomile:

I bless this chamomile to nurture tranquility and healing.
Help me reduce stress.

Add the chamomile to the sachet after it has been blessed by the white light. Take the rose quartz crystal into your palm and call on its energy:

I bless this rose quartz to purify and open the heart.
Help me promote self-love, compassion, deep inner healing, and feelings of peace.

Bless the rose quartz with the bright white light and place it into the sachet. Pull the drawstrings tight and tie them together three times, binding the sachet. Hold it in your hands, allowing everything to be blessed so the energies may work together for your purpose. When you are ready, remember to thank the guides you called upon and place the sachet under your pillow.

Coping with Loneliness Spell

To cope with loneliness, it is important to understand it. Loneliness feels like a hole in your soul as isolation eats away at your self – esteem. It can be overwhelming and feels like a bottomless pit. So, how do we find peace? By filling the hole with things that make us feel loved. Finding peace in loneliness is a challenge, but nothing is impossible. Chronic loneliness is a deep yearning for understanding, acceptance, belonging. Finding these within yourself is the first step toward peace.

Set the scene with:

- A light blue or white candle

- Pen and paper

- Lavender essential oil or a lavender – infused oil

Begin by dressing the candle toward you with the lavender oil while focusing on your intentions of finding peace and harmony. When you are ready, light the candle, speaking your intention aloud:

I seek peace within myself.
I look inward to find harmony.
I create a sense of belonging by belonging first to myself.

After speaking your intention, grab the pen and paper. Create a list of three things that fill your soul, including hobbies such as dancing, cooking, or reading your favorite book. Think of things which help you feel more like yourself. Anything that you genuinely enjoy. Next, write three ways that you can reach out to others. You can join a book club, reconnect with friends on social media, or sign up for volunteer work. Last, write down three positive affirmations reminding you to love yourself. You can use any of the affirmations listed earlier in this book or create custom affirmations that align with your intention.

Once your lists are ready, close your eyes. Reaffirm your intention as you imagine a bright light washing over you – whatever color feels most peaceful to you. Allow this light to cleanse you and be a source of comfort. This light is representative of your inner peace. Imagine this light filling the holes that you feel within your heart and soul, filling you with peace. Wrap your arms around yourself in a tight embrace. Be accepting and understanding of yourself and hold on until you are ready to release the energy.

After the working is complete, display your lists as a reminder to yourself. You can keep them on your altar or tape it to your bathroom mirror, anyplace that you will be able to refer back to easily. This is your checklist. Repeat the affirmations to yourself as often as you need. Remember to do the activities you love and enjoy. Act on different ways to reach out to others. Your work in the mundane world is just as important as your spiritual work; true growth requires both.

Coping with Loneliness Meditation

This meditation is a form of self-reflection, taking a deep look within as you fill your soul. This is a shorter meditation that can be repeated as often as you need. As with all meditations in this book, take time to prepare in advance. You can even make notes ahead of time to organize your thoughts and intentions. When you are ready, find a comfortable seat and close your eyes.

Find yourself in a garden. Look around, checking your surroundings. Notice the vegetation and the flowers. Listen to the sounds of the birds singing. Feel the wind blow through your hair. The sun is warm on your skin. What does your garden look like? How does your garden make you feel?

After you have explored the garden, you notice an empty planter off to the side. The planter is dirty, seemingly forgotten in the lush garden. Take some time here to clean the planter, revealing a beautiful pattern underneath. Do you use a hose? Is there water nearby? A pond? Fountain? You will also find a small pile of fertile soil with a small trowel at the base. A gardening table close by holds seeds and flowers. Take your time to fill the planter, adding either seeds or young flowers to grow and flourish. The soils will nourish whatever you choose to plant here, allowing it to grow and thrive. Make sure to water and nurture what you grow,

When you are ready, place the planter in the center of the garden. Watch as it miraculously grows and thrives until it is the strongest feature of your garden. Allow the roots to grow deep as the green leaves stretch toward the warm sun, full of life. This new plant attracts butterflies, birds, and deer. The garden grows stronger and more beautiful that it was before.

Remember to return to your garden as often as you need. Allow this to be a place of comfort and solace. Most importantly, remember to nourish your soul as you nourish your garden so you too may grow and thrive.

Coping with Loneliness Affirmations

Human beings are social creatures. We tend to need interaction with others to help maintain healthy relationships. When those interactions are limited for whatever reason, it affects us, often negatively. Loneliness can result from different traumatic events, including the death of a loved one, or as we have recently seen, a worldwide pandemic. These affirmations are to help remind us of the positive as we work through feelings of seclusion.

- I am never truly alone. The [universe/my deity] is with me.

- I am my best source of comfort; I allow myself to receive it.

- I attract people who value me. I attract people I value.

- I find the quiet peace in solitude.

- I am my own best friend.

- All I need is me.

Try combining affirmations together in different patterns and orders to create your own specialized wordings.

Coping with Loneliness Prayer

When in need of divine compassion, our deities are only words away. Reach out to your higher power with your healing requests. As usual, open your prayer according to your pathway, and then continue:

When I'm lonely, I come to you.
In search of compassion and peace.
While I understand I am enough,
Isolation takes a toll.
My heart aches for lost companionship.
I pray for what I need to be brought into my life,
To share a world of love.
To turn to when I am in need,
To know I am not alone.
Take my hand and guide me with love and compassion.
Guide me to find contentment.
Ease my loneliness and draw refuge to me.
Fill me with hope and bless me with the comfort I seek.

If you have a specific request or words of your own to say, do so now and then close your prayer as usual.

Journal Exercise

Give yourself the compassion you would give to others. It's ok to feel sad and lonely sometimes. The problem comes when we either deny these feelings or we can't move on from them. We get stuck. Problems occur when we don't heal.

If you are a people pleaser, or someone who has raised to look to others for praise and acceptance, you may experience loneliness on a deeper level. Learn to give yourself the praise and acceptance you seek from others.

How do you combat loneliness? Do your methods work? How can you show yourself compassion when loneliness creeps in?

Lavender Rose Hot Chocolate for Healing Heartache

They say that only time can mend a broken heart, but this lavender rose hot chocolate recipe is a bit of kitchen witchery to ease and heal the ache. Cacao has historically been used in Mayan and Aztec traditions to bring peace and open the heart. A mug of hot chocolate is the perfect comfort food to soothe heartache. For this recipe, we add rose buds for happiness and to nourish the heart, and lavender for peace, healing, and harmony.

For this recipe you will need:

- 1 cup of milk or nondairy milk alternative

- 1 tablespoon of organic food- grade rose buds or petals (any color)

- 1 teaspoon food-grade lavender buds

- 1/4 teaspoon vanilla extract

- 2 tablespoons cacao powder (alternatively cocoa powder can be used)

- Optional: 1 teaspoon honey

Take a moment to ground yourself before you begin, then set your intentions. Heat the milk or nondairy milk alternative on the stove with the rose and lavender, careful not to let it boil. Occasionally stir with a whisk, adding your own energy to work along with the cacao and flowers. Allow this to steep for 10 minutes. Turn off the heat and strain out the flowers. Add the remaining ingredients and use either a frother or whisk to mix again.

Grab a cozy blanket and sit in your favorite comfy spot. Close your eyes and take a sip, soothing your heart. Allow yourself to take this time to simply *be*.

Ritual for Rediscovering Yourself

Every day, we change. We are affected by the decisions we make and the experiences we live through, no matter how big or small they may appear to be. Whether is is recovering from trauma, learning coping mechanisms, or simply experiencing the chaos of our daily lives, we are impacted in profound ways. Sometimes, after all this change, we may no longer truly recognize who we are. This ritual will assist us in looking within to rediscover who we have become.

This ritual can be repeated as necessary or combined with the Mediation for Rediscovering Yourself. Soul searching is a journey. Take as much time as you need.

Set the scene with:

- A white or light blue candle

- A lighter or matches

- A mirror – any size will do

- A journal and something to write with

- Rose quartz

- Optional: Rosemary incense.

For this ritual you can sit in front of a mirror or use a smaller, handheld mirror. Any size is fine as long as you can see your entire face in the reflection. Begin this ritual by lighting the white or blue candle. You can call upon any guides or deities you work with to assist you in this working.

Take the rose quartz in the palm of your dominant hand. If your mirror is handheld, hold it in your other hand. Set your intentions, and you are ready, recite the following incantation:

> *Open my eyes so I can see,*
> *Who it is, I call me.*

Open your eyes. Hold the rose quartz to your heart and turn your gaze to the reflection in the mirror. The rose quartz is a stone for self-love and compassion. As you look upon yourself, take note of what you see, but do so with compassion for yourself. Focus first on your features – the line of your jaw, the angles of your nose, the fullness and curvature of your lips. Then turn to your eyes. Look beyond their shape and color – look within yourself.

When you are ready to start writing, set the rose quartz down and pick up your journal and writing utensil. Return your gaze to your reflection and allow yourself to free write what – or rather, who – you see looking back at you. Allow the words to flow freely and remember to use compassion with yourself. Not only is this a self-discovery ritual, it is also a self-love ritual.

Take as much time as you need to write without overthinking about what you are putting down. Let your thoughts go and simply write. This allows our intuition to take over, opening the doors to the parts of ourselves that often remain hidden.

When you feel that you have expressed all that you can, let the pen fall. Pick the rose quartz up once more, returning it to your heart. Smile at your reflection with compassion and acceptance.

Thank your guides and keep the rose quartz on your altar to complete this ritual. Return to your journal and reflect on what you had written during the intuitive freewriting exercise. Self-discovery is a process; return to this journal and repeat this ritual as often as needed.

Meditation for Rediscovering Yourself

Everything we experience in life- the ups and the downs – can impact who we are and how we see ourselves. Sometimes, we can lose sight of who we are. This meditation is designed for when you look in a mirror and you no longer recognize the face looking back at you. This mediation can be practiced as often as needed and used with the

Ritual for Rediscovering Yourself. Complete the trifecta by ending your practice with the affirmations included below this section.

This meditation is lengthy but simple in practice. To be fully prepared, I recommend reading the meditation several times in advance or record yourself reading the meditation aloud to give yourself a guide to work with when you are ready to practice.

In this meditation, you will be meeting different versions of yourself – the "you" that used to be, the "you" that has been burdened by chaos, and "you" that you wish to be. By meeting and morphing with each version of yourself, you are practicing self-acceptance, self-love, and self-discovery. You may want to have a journal and pen prepared for self-reflection after the meditation. As always, set aside uninterrupted time in a safe and comfortable space.

Close your eyes and allow yourself to be transported to a garden. Take a few moments to explore the details of the garden around you. Notice the colors and fragrance of the flowers. Feel the breeze on your face. Touch the grass and note how it feels against your fingertips. Pay attention to what sounds you hear. Are there any animals around you? Take as much time as you need here, allow this to be a place of comfort, warmth, and security. You are safe.

After you explore your garden, a path opens ahead of you. Take the first step forward in your journey and see where it takes you. Are you still in the garden? Where does it lead?

Keep walking until you see someone ahead of you. As you come closer and their face becomes focused, you realize the person is you – or rather, a version of you. Meet the "you" that you used to be, someone who was happy, before trauma or chaos. Gaze upon this other you This figure may look remarkably younger, less bothered by the burdens that you have carried. Notice their features, their strengths, their weaknesses. Reach out and pull them into a tight embrace. As you hug other you, imagine that they are morphing into you, becoming one with you. You may not see this version of yourself anymore, but they are a part of who you are within. Allow this version of you to be a source of comfort.

As you move forward again, preparing to meet the next version of yourself, take note of your surroundings, particularly if there are any changes in the scenery. Continue walking until you meet the "you" that has been burdened by chaos. Notice their features, their strengths, and their weaknesses. How do you feel seeing this version of yourself? Take note of any emotions or thoughts that come up, then let them go. These feelings can be reflected on after the meditation is complete. When you are ready, reach forward to this other you and envelop them in a deep hug. Allow yourself to take them into you. Your burdens, your trauma, and experiences are all a part of you. Allow this version of you to be a source of strength.

Continue forward on your path. Return your attention to your surroundings. Remember, you are safe here. There is one more version of yourself for you to meet. When you are ready, welcome the "you" that you wish to become. Notice their features, their strengths, their weaknesses. What do you feel when you see this version of you? Reach forward and take this version into you just as you have done with the others. The person that you wish to be is already a part of who you are. Allow this version of you to be a source of confidence.

Now that you have met and embraced these other versions of you, it is time to reach the destination on this journey. Walk to the end of the path until you see a pool, pond, or well of clear water. Reach the water and look down to see your reflection. Now that you have embraced these other versions of yourself and accepted them as a part of who you are, what do you see when you look at your reflection? Take as much time as you need here. Notice your features, your strengths, and your weaknesses. See your comfort, your strength, and your confidence. Each of these versions are a part of your true self. When you put them all together, who are you?

When you are ready, open your eyes. Wrap your arms around yourself in a tight embrace. Hold yourself if you need. After you let go, turn to your journal. Reflect on your journey, Write down everything that you remember about the different versions of yourself that you met in meditation. All these versions of yourself are simply various aspects of who you are. By meeting each of them in meditation, you rediscover who you are.

Affirmations for Rediscovering Yourself

Relearning who you are, changing who you are, deciding who you want to be – all are within the realm of possibility and an important part of your spiritual journey. Let these affirmations remind you of who you are each step of the way.

- I know who I am.

- I accept change from within.

- I live as my authentic self.

- I am who I am meant to be.

- I embrace every aspect of myself.

- My inner truth speaks, and I listen.

- I speak my truth and the universe listens.

- My past changes me but does not define me.

- Every day I grow into the person I am meant to be.

- I am me.

As always, remember you can use each of these affirmations alone, or combine them together to create more complex groupings.

A Prayer for Rediscovering Yourself

A key step to self-discovery is to always speak your truth. They say, "The truth will set you free," and that holds true here as well. Speaking your truth allows you to live and express yourself authentically, and this helps you to discover who you truly are. We are always changing, growing, and adapting to the world around us. If we continue to speak our truth, we will always know who we truly are. These prayers serve as a simple reminder as we call upon our guides, deities, or the universe to assist in the path to self-discovery.

Since the goal is to speak your truth, these prayers do not have to be followed exactly as written. If you feel the need to say something out to the universe, trust that instinct. That is your inner truth waiting to be expressed. This script serves as a starting point to help inspire you. You are encourage to always add to your own individualized touch and speak from the heart. Remember this from the affirmations for rediscovering yourself: I speak my truth and the world listens. The world is listening to your prayer, so go ahead and speak your truth.

When you are ready to begin, open your prayer in whatever way best suits your personal practice, and then continue:

Every day I change and grow,
Every day I wonder.

I find myself changed,
and sometimes I don't recognize who I truly am.
I am ready to speak my truth,
Please, let the world listen.

During this prayer, you may find different thoughts or feelings popping into your head. Make notes of these to journal about and reflect on – these are a part of your inner truth. Self-discovery is often intuitive. Revelations can happen when we let go of control and trust our instincts.

Magical self-care has really made a major impact on wellness and how we deal with all that we experience in life. These practices have brought us many new tools to assist in coping with the challenges and struggles we face every day. Working with these practices helps us with inner healing, developing healthy coping mechanisms, and discovering new things about ourselves, all of which prepare us for the next chapter of this book: shadow work.

Chapter 9
Shadow Work

Where there is light, there must also be darkness. Like night and day, the yin and yang. The two naturally go together as counterparts. Where one is expected, the other will follow. Even the brightest room can disguise nooks and crannies where darkness lies hidden. We all have our own nooks and crannies where darkness lies hidden too. These dark aspects to our personalities may be things we don't always show or may not even be aware we have. These dark aspects combined are known as your shadow shelf.

The shadow is the parts of you that you don't always see, as they are often buried beneath the surface. These are the emotions that we try to stuff down because we view them as negative or inferior: rage, jealousy, regret, greed, selfishness, desire for power, etc. Since we view these things as negative, we cut ourselves off from them, effectively burying parts of our personality. This dissociation creates a split deep within us, leaving a part of us fragmented and forgotten.

The shadow cannot be eliminated, only repressed. Every time a feeling is repressed, the shadow grows. Repression can be dangerous, as some things can only be buried so deep. The shadow self can easily be triggered, leading to involuntary outbursts of anger or other actions that leave you feeling quite unlike your "normal" self.

The shadow is not only made of negative traits. There are many times when positive aspects of our personalities – such as strength and confidence – are suppressed. When we are silenced, our accomplishments ridiculed, or deemed to be "too much" by others, we suppress amazing parts of ourselves to suit others. By doing so, we continue to feed our shadow. The shadow self must be addressed and faced to move forward in your journey. This brings use to shadow work.

Shadow work is a form of psychoanalysis pioneered by twentieth-century Swiss psychologist Carl Jung. He believed that true balance and harmony could only be achieved by decompartmentalizing these repressed aspects of ourselves and reintegrating them with the rest of our personality. Jung addressed the shadow within himself in his book *Modern Man in Search of a Soul,* saying "How can I be substantial if I do not cast a shadow? I must have a dark side also if I am to be whole."[1]

Taking care of yourself requires treating your shadow self. Light and love is only one side of the coin. You must acknowledge your shadow, understand it, and learn from it to truly heal. The shadow is not something to fear, nor is it something to feel shame over. As Jung says in *Psychology and Alchemy,* "There is no light without shadow and psychic wholeness without imperfection." [2]

Approaching Shadow Work

There are many ways to approach shadow work. Working with a licensed professional therapist is highly encouraged, especially if there

---

1. Carl G. Jung, *Modern Man in Search of a Soul* (London: Routledge and Kegan Paul, 1933). 35.

2. Carl G. Jung. *Psychology and Alchemy* (London: Routledge and Kegan Paul, 1953), 152.

is any unresolved trauma. It is also recommended to have a developed healthy coping mechanisms in place for when preparing to meet your shadow.

Journaling, creative works, meditation, and spell work can all be used in shadow work, in addition to therapy. When it comes to shadow work, use the methods that work best for you and your own personal practice.

Before you begin shadow work, there are a few tips to help ensure a more beneficial experience.

- Release self-judgment. Shadow work requires you to be vulnerable with yourself. Treat yourself with compassion and kindness, or else you will only continue to feed your shadow.

- Ask why. To get to the root of those new emotions, it is important to ask why you are feeling a particular way. Addressing why you feel a certain way will help you discover where the feeling came from so that you can heal from it.

- Be honest. Honesty is the best policy, and it is a major component of shadow work. If you cannot be truly honest with yourself, you will not be able to move forward.

- Take your time. You cannot process everything all at once. Take your time. Shadow work does not need to be done daily, in fact it should not be. There are no deadlines, so there is no reason to rush. Take as much time as you need to process, heal, and recover before moving forward. Have patience with yourself.

- Be prepared. When it is time to address your shadow, make sure you are in a comfortable and safe space where you will not be interrupted. It is important to be centered and focused. Have a journal ready to record your thoughts and experiences. A glass of water or a box of tissues may be helpful.

- Aftercare. After doing any shadow work, it is important that you take the time to ground yourself. Allow yourself to come back to the present moment and spend time taking care of yourself. Self-love and self-acceptance are the root of shadow work.

Tools for Shadow Work

When doing shadow work, there are many magical tools that can assist you in your practice: herbs, stones and crystals, a journal for recording thoughts and experiences, or a mirror for self reflection.

Shadow work herbs can be burned as incense, left as offerings, or sealed in a sachet or spell jar. Additionally, they can be used in the form of essential oils, which can be diffused in an aromatherapy diffuser or diluted with a carrier oil and applied topically. Here are our favorite herbs for assisting with shadow work and their metaphysical properties:

- Garden sage promotes clarity and spiritual wisdom and cleanses negativity and fear.

- Rosemary enhances memory and concentration.

- Lavender relieves stress by fostering peace and harmony, which improves mental wellness and allows for a restful sleep.

- Chamomile promotes tranquility and relieves stress by soothing tension.

- Eucalyptus is used for cleansing, healing, and warding for protection before, during, and after shadow work.

- Lemongrass is uplifting and revitalizing, and it is useful in recovery after shadow work.

Stones and crystals are useful tools for shadow work as well as the recovery process. They can be placed on the body, held during meditation, or placed in front of or around you. Here are our favorite stones and crystals for assisting with shadow work and their metaphysical properties.

- Black obsidian helps us to see our shadows and promotes healing by helping to dissolve blockages that could be holding us back. It reveals our inner truth by acting as a mirror to the soul.

- Snowflake obsidian works very similar to black obsidian regarding revealing our shadow self and helps us attain freedom as we break the chains holding us down. The black and white design promotes balance between light and dark.

- Labradorite can be used to stimulate forgotten memories and break down illusions. As it strengthens intuition, we can look deeper within ourselves to seek the truth. Labradorite is great for revealing hidden patterns for self-reflection.

- Lapis lazuli encourages self-awareness and self-expression, and it helps with facing the truth. This stone is used to promote wisdom, balance, and emotional healing.

- Sodalite is known as "the truth stone" and encourages self-acceptance by helping to release self-judgment as we reveal the suppressed parts of our personalities.

- Black tourmaline is a protection stone used for deep grounding. It encourages objective and logical thought processes while relieving tension and dispelling fear and anger.

- Selenite is used for cleansing and protection. It promotes reconnection between your two selves and cleanses negativity. Selenite pairs nicely with black tourmaline.

- Amethyst bestows spiritual wakefulness by connecting the mind, body, and spirit. This is a great stone for meditation, as it encourages inner peace and helps to quiet the mind. Amethyst is also used as support for overcoming grief and loss.

- Rose quarts ignites self-love and compassion and helps improve self-esteem and body image. This helps us alleviate our worries and negative thoughts and feelings to help heal the heart.

Journaling is an important part of shadow work. It allows us to use our voice and fully express our thoughts and feelings. Recording our shadow work sessions also allows us to more easily evaluate hidden patterns that may have been missed otherwise. There are many shadow work prompts for journaling exercises. Even when doing shadow work through spells, rituals, and meditations, having a written account afterward may be beneficial to your practice.

A mirror is also a great tool for shadow work, as the eyes are the window to the soul. Sometimes to look within, we need to look at ourselves. When using a mirror in shadow work, it is important to practice non-judgement. To heal the shadow self, we must be fully accepting of all aspects of who we are. Non-judgment can be challenging but it is vital.

Although shadow work is extremely important for your spiritual journey and will in fact be a great deal of your travels, it must be emphasized this type of work is not to be entered into lightly. Encountering the shadow without proper coping skills can be detrimental. If you are serious and attentive to yourself, you will know when you are ready to meet your darker side. If you do not feel ready, you are not ready. It is that simple. Do not let anyone push you into work you are not ready for. Social media is filled with misinformation. I can't tell you how many times I have seen posts in groups or videos of people pushing others into shadow work using intimidation. This is a red flag – if someone is using intimidation to push shadow work, don't listen to them. Threats of, "You will never get anywhere without it" are meant to scare you and get them views. Shadow work is an incredibly personal journey. No one can tell you when you are equipped for the journey better than you can. No one can take your journey for you. It is for you and you alone.

Because shadow work involves revealing the hidden, this means revisiting past traumas. It can also mean remembering or recognizing past traumas for the first time. This can be deeply painful work. Be ready for it.

Shadow work takes preparation. The rest of this chapter includes spells, rituals, meditations, and journaling prompts for when you are ready to begin.

Cord Cutting Ritual

A cord cutting ritual is a powerful tool for energetically cutting ties to other people, unpleasant situations, or even negative traits within ourselves. This helps to finalize severing physical and mental connections in the mundane world and is a wonderful way to enter the realm of shadow work. As we cut ties with negative or toxic things around us, we can begin to look inward and reflect on ourselves.

Set the scene with:

- Two taper or chime candles, preferably white or one white and one black

- A safety pin

- A flammable cord or string, about nine inches long

- A lighter

- Firesafe plate or tray

- White salt

- Journal and pen

Before beginning this ritual, the candles will need to be prepared. Using the safety pin, you will carve your name longways down the side of the first candle. If using two different colored candles, the white one will be the first candle. For the second candle, or the black candle, you will carve the name of whoever – or whatever- it is that you are looking to cut ties with. Once the candles are prepared, take the cord or string and wrap it around the first candle three times. Leave some slack and wrap the other end around the second candle, also three times. Each candle will be wrapped by the connecting cord as a representation of the energetic connection.

Place the connected candles on a firesafe plate or tray and encircle them with a ring of white salt. Be sure the ring of salt is large enough both candles fit inside. The circle does not have to be perfect but try to make it as even as you can.

When you are ready, call upon any higher power or spirit guides to assist you in this working and set your intention. Focus on each candle for a moment, close your eyes, and see in your mind what each candle represents to you. After your intentions are set, light the wick of each candle, starting with your candle. You can speak your intentions aloud, ask for the energetic connections to be served as the cord burns away, or sit in quiet reflection.

As the candles burn down, the cord will eventually catch fire and burn away. (Keep a close eye on the cord and flame to ensure your safety. Do not leave this ritual unattended for any reason.) Allow the cord and both the candles to burn out completely before ending your working. Follow up with your journal, reflecting on these questions and anything else you wish to record:

- What steps did you take to server this connection in the mundane world?

- What will you do to ensure this connection remains severed?

- What did you feel in your body as the cords were severed?

- What does severing this connection mean to you?

- What aspects of your shadow were revealed to you while completing this ritual?

- How will you heal and care for yourself moving forward?

Cord Cutting Meditation

If the required materials for the cord cutting ritual are not available to you, it is possible to cut energetic ties through meditation instead of spell work. Cord cutting meditations are just as effective and are a firesafe option. This meditation can be completed in addition to the ritual or repeated on your own as often as you desire. The cord cutting meditation is quite simple in nature and easily customizable to best suit your needs.

When you are ready to begin, close your eyes and center yourself, align with your intention. See yourself sitting in a comfortable room. Have a look around and notice the subtle details around you. Know that you are safe here in this space. Look across from you. On the other side of the room, you see the person or situation to which you are connected. Take your time, see the details. If this is a person, imagine their face, their clothes, their voice. Notice what they are doing. If the connection is a situation, allow yourself to see the scene play over and over. Whatever it is you want to cut ties with, focus on the details to see it very clearly on the other side of the room.

However, please note that for some events or people, you may not want to see their face or don't care to repeat the event in your mind even once, and definitely not over and over. This is completely understandable. In these situations, I prefer to visualize the offender as a black void. A blank space that I can shrink down to whatever size I wish. Remember, you can use symbolic representations when you want to.

Once you have a clear picture or a void in mind, imagine a large, thick, black rope wrapping around your waist. The rope crosses the room and continues to wrap its way around on the other side. For a moment, you are trapped, tied to the other side.

Take a pair of large scissors in your hand and begin to cut away at the black cord. See the cord fall away and the wrapping drop, You are free. The other side of the room begins to fall away; the connection has been severed. See yourself as you wish to be without this connection holding you back and return from your meditative state.

Letter to your Shadow Self

Writing is a cathartic practice that helps unleash hidden emotions as we express the deepest part of ourselves. This practice is a form of shadow work which can be repeated often and customized to suit your specific needs and desires. The concept is simple – we are writing letters to our shadow selves in a safe and comfortable environment. There is no right or wrong way to conduct this freewriting exercise if you are authentic, honest, and free of self-judgments. The fist step is to ensure you are comfortable and have a stretch of uninterrupted alone time – we can more easily and more honestly connect with our shadow selves when we are alone. It is easier to let go of judgments when we do not feel any outside pressure.

Set the scene with:

- Pen and paper

- Optional: a lighter or match and a fireproof container.

- Optional: a shovel and pot or soil or space with dirt outdoors

You can write as many letters as you choose but allow each letter to focus on just one aspect of your shadow self. As you write, explore the specific trait you are choosing to focus on. Speak to this part of you. Discover where this shadow came from; what act of suppression caused you to repress this part of you? How can you unbury and release it? How can you heal this part of you, connect with it, and move forward? Do not hold back any emotions; write everything, even the things that may be hard for your to admit to yourself.

Freewriting allows us to express the parts of ourselves we keep hidden. Self-expression helps to unbury the shadow. Practicing non-judgment and forgiveness heals the shadow. Processing and moving forward allows you to integrate the shadow in a healthy and positive manner.

After you have finished writing, take the time to read the whole letter. Sometimes the words may surprise you. Notice how these words make you feel. Use this as a chance to truly get to know your shadow. When you are ready, there are a couple of options available for the next step. The letter can either be burned in a fireproof container or it can be buried in the earth, where it will eventually break down. Either method can be used to release the shadow.

Whichever option you choose to release the letter, take a moment of silence afterward. Turn your attention inward. Pay attention to any area that feel heavy. Send love, healing, and forgiveness to these areas. Wrap your arms around yourself in a tight embrace. Stay here as long as you need. Self- love is vital to shadow work.

Out with the Old and In with the New Ritual

This is a two part ritual designed for letting go of negative behaviors and old patterns while paving the way for a stronger and more empowered you. It's time to dive deep and dust the cobwebs off the dark corners of your soul to reflect on the parts of yourself that you keep hidden. With this working, you can embody the traits and qualities that you desire to create a profound transformation.

For this ritual you will create two custom herbal mixes, one for banishing and one for empowerment. There are numerous herbs for these purposes; build your blend based on what is available to you. Recommended herbs for a banishing mix are nettle, agrimony, black pepper, mullein, juniper berries, and onion powder or dried minced onion. For the empowerment blend, you can use any mix of the following herbs: celandine, chili pepper, cinnamon, fennel, sandalwood, blessed thistle, cedar, or motherwort.

Set the scene with:

- A white candle

- A fireproof container

- A self lighting charcoal tablet

- A lighter

- Pen and at least two pieces of paper

- Banishing herb mix

- Empowerment herb mix

- A spoon or scoop

Ground and center yourself and prepare the self-lighting charcoal tablet. If you work with any guides or deities, feel free to call upon them for their assistance and to watch over you during this ritual. When you are ready, light the white candle and speak your intention:

I come to let go and release so that I may step forth

with renewed strength, clarity and empowerment.

Take the first piece of paper. Reflect on negative behaviors, old patters, self-doubt, and anything that holds you back. Begin to write, "I let go of..." and list each quality, one at a time. You can write as little or as much as you want. Feel free to be as descriptive as you like and hold nothing back. Once you are ready, fold the paper three times away from you to banish these behaviors. Light the corner of the paper with the flame of the white candle and drop it into the fireproof container, saying:

I release that which no longer serves me.

As is my will, so mote it be.

As the paper burns, carefully scoop the banishing mix into the fire. Focus on your intention; allow these behaviors, thoughts, patterns, and attitudes to leave you. When the paper has burned and the flame dies down, move on the second piece of paper.

On this paper, write down intentions that empower you. Write what you want to attract, list the attitudes and behaviors you want to develop, and include the new patterns you would like to build. Be as detailed as you like. At the end of the list, write "I am empowered to be who I am." Fold the paper three times, this time toward you to bring these things to you. Once again, light the corner of the paper with the flame of the white candle and drop it into the fireproof container, saying:

I attract only that which will serve me,
As is my will, so mote it be.

As the paper burns, safely scoop the empowerment herb mix into the fire. Focus on your intention; see yourself building new patterns, transforming into a more empowered you. When the embers have fully burned and it is safe to move them, scatter the ashes to the wind, finalizing your intention with these words:

I arise from the ashes anew, renewed, and empowered,
As is my will, so mote it be

Journal Exercise

Journal about your experience. What did you release? What do you want to attract? Revisit this entry in a few weeks to see how you are doing.

Healing Your Inner Child Meditation

Healing your inner child is an extremely crucial step within shadow work. When we are young, we often suppress many things to seek approval and praise from our peers as well as from adults in our life. As we grow older, these aspects of ourselves that we spent so many years suppressing build up in our shadow selves. As we work to understand and positively integrate our shadow selves, our inner child is left vulnerable. Through this mediation, we will connect with our inner child and provide them with the love and care they need to heal. This meditation can be repeated as needed, but it is reserved to be one of the final shadow work activities in this book. As always, prepare your meditation in advance and ensure you have a comfortable space where you will not be interrupted.

As we begin this meditation and set our intentions, let us close our eyes and imagine ourselves in a peaceful garden. This may be the same meditative garden that we have worked with in past meditations, or you can imagine an entirely new garden. Wherever you are, take a moment to notice the sights around you. Smell the flora, hear the birds sing, feel the grass beneath your feet.

After you familiarize yourself with your garden, look ahead of you to find your inner child. Your inner child often resembles a version of you when you were younger. Notice what your inner child is doing. Are they enjoying a picnic? Playing in the sand? Swinging on a swing set or coloring a picture? What activity are they engaging in, and what emotions are they feeling? What does their area of the garden look like? In what ways is it like the rest of the garden? In what ways is it different?

When you are ready, join your inner child in their area of the garden. If they are coloring, you can color too. If they are swinging on a swing set, give them a gentle push from behind. Take some time simply being with your inner child. Give them the attention that they deserve from you. As you spend time together, feel free to open a dialogue with your inner child. You can ask what it is they need, what do they want to do, and how they feel. Truly listen and communicate with your inner child and be sure to follow through with what you say. Let your inner child feel heard and show them they are loved and appreciated. Give them the care you needed as a child and love them in the way that you needed to be loved. Allow them to be a child doing things kids like to do – the things that we no longer do when we become adults. Most importantly, allow them to be their authentic selves with no pressure to suppress any part of themselves.

Spend as much time as you need with your inner child, showing them love and encouraging them to be their authentic self. When you are ready, be sure to wrap your arms around your inner child and hold them in a tight embrace before leaving your garden. As you return to the present moment, wrap your arms around yourself and hold yourself in a tight embrace, just as you did with your inner child in meditation. Know that your inner child is still a part of you that deserves love and care. Self-love and self-care include loving and caring for your inner child instead of suppressing them in favor of adulthood.

Journal Exercise

Journal about your meditation. What did your inner child need? What did you give them? How did you spend your time together? What feelings did you share?

Aftercare and Recovery

Shadow work can be a physically, mentally, and emotionally draining process. It is normal to feel exhausted after shadow work. Aftercare is vital for a healthy recovery. There are many ways to practice aftercare to recover from shadow work: drinking plenty of water, eating a grounding meal, or taking a relaxing bath with bath salts are just a few examples. An effective aftercare process needs to ground our energy, nourish our body, and comfort us with self-love and self-care.

Hydrating Moon Water

Moon water is a common tool used in many witchcraft practices for spell work and manifestation due to its concentration of lunar energy and properties of spiritual transformation and blessing. Moon water can also be used to hydrate and bless the body when recovering after shadow work. This is one of the simplest recipes in this book, but it is filled with intention and power.

For this recipe you will need:

- At least 16 ounces of drinkable water in a closed, transparent container or bottle

- Access to the moon (either outside in a safe location, or inside on a window ledge)

After the full moon rises, simply place your container of water under the moonlight and set your intentions. You can place crystals or herbs around the water n(but not in it; water is bad for some stones and crystals and may be toxic to drink), ask for blessings from your guides or deities, or recite an incantation or affirmation. It does not need to charge all night, even just two hours is fine. Direct access to moonlight is not necessary, so do not worry if the sky is overcast.

When to retrieve your moon-charged water depends on your personal practice. Some practices focus more on the intention, so it is okay if the water is not brought in until after the sun has risen. Other practices hold the belief that moon water should never touch the light of day. This is entirely up to you, so do what works best for your own practice.

Drinking this water after shadow work practice will provide an extra energetic boost to cleanse, refresh, and bless your mind and spirit while hydrating your body.

Nourishing Nettle Infusion

Stinging nettle is used in metaphysical and magical practices for protection and to assist in blocking negativity. Additionally, culinary-grade dried stinging nettle leaf can be used to create a nourishing herbal tonic that is high in vitamin K and fuels the body with trace minerals and antioxidants. For an additional magic boost, you can use moon water.

Herbal infusions are different from your standard cup of tea. Herbal teas use a small amount of herbs that are steeped for only about 3-5 minutes. An herbal infusion is a tonic consisting of a larger amount of herbs steeped for a minimum of four hours and for up to 24 hours.

For this recipe you will need:

- 16 ounces of boiling water in a pot with a lid

- 4 ounces of sifted or cut culinary-grade dried stinging nettle

- A pitcher or 1 pint mason jar with lid

- A piece of cheesecloth or mesh strainer

- Sweetener of choice for taste

Once the water starts to boil, turn the stove off and remove the pot from the heat. Add the stinging nettle, place the lid on, and allow the mixture to infuse for at least 4 hours. If you intend to allow the infusion to steep for longer than four hours, you may want to move it to the refrigerator for freshness. Strain the mixture and dispose of the herbs when transferring to a pitcher or a mason jar, and then the infusion is ready to drink. The infusion will last up to 3 days in the refrigerator.

The stinging nettle infusion has a very earthy taste. The flavor is great for grounding but may be bitter on its own. Add your favorite sweetener for taste – honey, sugar, maple syrup, or agave nectar are popular choices.

Grounding Cheese Board

It is important to ground after workings that use our energy, and shadow work is no exception. Food is a wonderful way to fuel our body while providing a comforting and grounding experience. A French – inspired cheese board is easily customizable for dietary and preferences (there are even many vegan cheeses available).

For this recipe you will need:

- At least 3 kinds of cheese or nondairy cheese alternative

- Fresh or dried fruit

- Sliced Vienna bread, crostini, or crackers

- A selection of your favorite nuts and seeds

- A piece of your favorite chocolate or candy

- Optional: Sliced meats such as salami, prosciutto, pepperoni, or something more traditional such as turkey or roast beef.

- A wooden board or platter large enough to fit your selection

There is no wrong way to lay out a cheeseboard. Feel free to include as many or as few options as you like. Cheese boards are great for experimenting, so add something new that you have always wanted to try! You can keep it simple with a few of your favorites or create a complex masterpiece combining new and bold flavors.

Your cheeseboard can be prepared i n advance before your shadow work session, leave it in the refrigerator until you are ready. When putting your cheeseboard together, you may want to use of the food prep blessings provided earlier in this book. Allow the cheeseboard to be a spiritual experience.

Cleansing Aftercare Meditation with Purification Bath Salts

As we know, the bathtub is a perfect location for cleansing not just physically but mentally, emotionally, and spiritually as well. This cleansing aftercare meditation with purification bath salts provides a magical meditative experience to help wash away the heaviness felt after shadow work. This meditation is a ritualistic experience.

You may create a spa-like ambience by lighting white candles or playing some quiet, relaxing music – whatever will help you feel re-laxed and comfortable.

Purification Bath Salts

Adding these bath salts to any bath will cleanse and purify the mind and spirit as you cleanse your body.

For these bath salts you will need:

- 1 cup of any combination of bath salts: Epsom salts, sea salt, pink Himalayan salt

- 1/2 tablespoon dried blessed thistle

- 1/2 tablespoon dried hyssop

- 1/2 tablespoon dried culinary sage

- 1/2 tablespoon dried peppermint

- A bowl and spoon or spatula for mixing

- Any 8 ounce jar with a lid

- Optional: colloidal oatmeal for baths

Combine all the ingredients in a bowl and mix until well combined, then transfer into a jar that has a lid. Depending on how much you choose to use, this mixture should last 2 – 4 baths.

Cleansing Aftercare Meditation

For this meditative practice, prepare the bath water with bath salts before you step in. Use your hand or even a large kitchen spoon to stir the bathwater counterclockwise three times as you set your intention and recite the following:

I banish negative energy from myself and this space,

I release that which does not serve me.

Now stir the bath water clockwise three times and say:
I am cleansed as this space is cleansed,
I purify my body, my mind, and my spirit.

Enter the bathtub, taking a moment to get settled and comfortable. Close your eyes and take ten slow, deep breaths. With each inhale, imagine a bright, white light filling your body from top to bottom. Exhale, release, and allow the light to wash away any negativity you feel. Pay special attention to any areas that feel especially heavy or dark and send extra purifying energy there. If you feel ten breaths is not enough, take as much time as you need.

After energetically cleansing with the bright, white light, open your eyes so that you can safely move into a standing position. When you are ready, get your washcloth or loofah – whatever you used when bathing. This time, starting from the bottom of your feet and slowly working upward, physically cleanse every part of your body, washing three times counterclockwise, then three times clockwise again. If you choose, you can repeat the same incantations used to bless the bathwater.

Continue moving this way until you get to the top of your head. Close your eyes and squeeze the water out over your head, allowing the water to drip down your body before ending your bath.

Shadow work is a deeply personal practice that can look different for everyone. There are no timelines when it comes to shadow work. Some start shadow work early in their practice, while others may wait until they are deep in their practice before connecting with their shadow side. The most important facet of shadow work is doing what is best for you and your own practice. What works for some may not work for others. Take what you need and leave the rest. A strong shadow work practice is dependent upon stability. If at any time a shadow work ritual, meditation, or activity triggers a negative experience, unresolved trauma, or uncovers a new hidden trauma, it is important to seek professional help. Shadow work comes from therapy, and sometimes we must return to that foundation before moving forward.

Chapter 10
Healing Others

We live, play, and work in many different types of societies, and this can mean many different issues that may need healing. From smaller localized societies, such as your coven or family, to larger broader societies, such as your country and the world, we have learned healing needs to take place everywhere. Healing is what allows us to move forward and evolve to a higher level. In this last chapter, we will share spells and rituals to heal a variety of social issues. When appropriate, these rituals can be adjusted for group use. When we perform ritual in a group, the multiple energies feed off each other, allowing for a greater energy buildup and shifting. Group work multiplies power and energy exponentially.

Ritual to Heal Your Family

Some family traumas can be worked through, keeping a family intact. Others, not so much. It is important to point out healing your family is not the same thing as bringing your family together in agreement. Healing does not necessarily mean a family will be brought back together, nor stay in place. It means each person in the family deserves healing. Healing may include boundaries including physical distance, emotional distance, or both between the members. This ritual is to heal each of the people involved, not bend them to a will they do not wish to be bent to.

If possible, the family should perform this ritual together, if not, it's okay. You can send out healing energies to any family members who are unable to be present but are willing to work the ritual with you. Family members who do not know this is happening, should not be included. Respecting wishes may bring additional healing later.

Each person will need to prepare a letter ahead of time. Family members who are not physically present may send in a letter. This letter should be sealed in an envelope and not read by anyone. In your letter, write out a list of your grievances with your family members. What do you feel was done to you? How do you feel you were harmed? No one else will see your letter, so write freely from the heart. Whether you have discussed these matters with the involved family members or not, write it all down. Getting it down onto paper is a way to physically remove these issues from your body. Let them go as the ink flows across the paper. Release any pain, anxiety, or other negative feelings these grievances hold on you. We are not "forgiving and forgetting" in this letter; your intention is to remove some of the built-up, pent-up negative energy these issues have brought with them. Removing this negative energy is necessary for each individual member of the family to heal. It is necessary for everyone to heal for the family to heal. If you feel your brother was an asshole, say so, but also say why. What actions were done (or not done) that affected your feelings? You can give specifics or just generalizations, such as physically or mentally abusive. Again, as you write, you want to focus on pulling negative energy out and pushing it into the paper. Seal it into an envelope when you are done.

Set the scene with:

- A safe way to burn. This may mean an indoor fireplace, an

outdoor bonfire, or the inside of a cauldron or other fire-proof container. Because of the amount of paper you are burning, this part needs to be done outside if you are not using an indoor fireplace. Otherwise, you run the risk of setting off smoke detectors.

- Matches or lighter

- A brown chime or taper candle for each participant, along with a safe way to hold them to protect everyone from hot dripping wax. We use brown as it not only symbolizes family issues, but it also corresponds with decision-making (we are deciding to let go of negativity), grace, and strength. It is also a color for grounding and neutrality. These correspond with ridding our systems of negative energy.

- The following dried herbs: Angelica, Balm of Gilead, dandelion, horehound, nettle, and pine needles

- Ribbon strips of birch bark

How much of each of these you need will depend on how many people will be taking part in the ritual. You will combine these ingredients together to form an incense blend. Each participant should have about 2 tablespoons to work with. You can either give each person a small bowl with theirs in it or have everyone take from one community bowl during the ritual. Just make sure there is enough to go around for everyone.

If everyone is willing, you can mix the herbs into the incense together, taking turns adding ingredients and, if available, using a mortar and pestle to grind then finer. As the the ingredients are combined, everyone's intention should be on creating an incense that will help to release negative energies.

When you are ready to perform the ritual, everyone should assume a position around the fire or fireproof container. If you are inside with a fireplace, spread out in front of it. If you are comfortable with it, hold hands.

Everyone say together:

We come together, to help one another heal.
We are of the same blood, but we are not of the same mind.
Our past together has caused pain.
As a family, we release the pain.
We wish healing for ourselves.
We wish healing for each other.

If you held hands, you may drop them now. Each person should light their brown candle.

Take turns according to birth date, not age. In the case of multiple births on the same day, break it down by time of birth. The person whose birthday is closest to January 1st goes first, moving progressively through the year. Hold the lit candle in your dominant (or power) hand and the letter in the other. Say:

I release that which does not serve me.
I set this energy free.

Light the envelope with the brown candle and toss it either into the fire or fireproof container you are using. Be sure to light the envelope first. You want to ensure you and the brown candle are the connective reason the energy goes up in cleansing flames. Follow up with incense. If you are using a bonfire or fire place, toss your incense into the flames. If you are using a fireproof container, very gently, and carefully sprinkle bits of incense on your envelope as it burns. It will be more difficult to burn in a container, so carefully relight the papers with your candle if necessary. Visualize the cleansing of the energy as you watch your offering burn. Your turn does not end until your papers are completely burned. Once they are ash, extinguish your candle.

Allow each person their moment. It is imperative everyone remains respectful and silent for each other, holding space. If there are people not present but their letters are, someone should light the envelope and complete the process for them.

When everyone is finished, you may hold hands again if you wish. Say:

> *We release this energy through cleansing fire.*
> *Healing thoughts we do inspire.*

Depending on the dynamics in your family, you may want to end this ritual right away and go your separate ways. Or you may want to stand around the fire for a while, soaking in the warming energy of the flames. Either response is acceptable.

Energy Raising Ritual for a Cause

Need good vibes before a peaceful protest? Are you getting ready for a charity walk or 5K run? Launching a letter writing campaign? Planning to write and promote a new petition? You can use this adaptable ritual for any supportive, community-centered event. It does not matter which cause you are working with, use this ritual to build energy and set your intentions. This ritual is not about the event itself; it is all about raising energy for the event.

This energy raising is not only intended for political or community service based projects, but can also be performed before a wedding or handfasting ceremony, for a baby shower, to kick off a parade, honor the opening of a new community park, or even at the start of a pride themed event, such as a Pagan Pride festival.

There is a lot of preparation needed for this ritual, however it is completely customizable to suit your needs. For versatility, this is designed for both solitary practices as well as group based workings.

This is a two part working, In the first part, we will design and create energy raising shakers to use in the energy raising process. This is an art project which can be a ritualistic experience itself. You can call upon your guides, meditate beforehand, create sacred space, raise energy, and enchant and charge the tools and materials that you will be using.

The materials listed here including many optional items, there is no wrong way to make an energy raising shaker as long as it makes some noise. For this project you can be as creative as you like. Use the materials that are available to you or think outside of the box and try something new. This is a great project for recycling too – you can use empty water bottles, old vitamin or prescription bottles, a leftover Pringles can, or a milk jug. Search for any kind of unique container and experiment with different sizes, shapes, and textures to make different sounds.

For this project you will need:

- Empty container that can be sealed (cardboard salt cans work great too)

- Masking tape to seal the container if necessary

- markers or paint and paintbrushes

- various dried beans, small pebbles, rice and other small, noisy items

To begin, remove all labels from the container you use and ensure it's clean. Open the top and fill the container with any small items that can make noise. We used dried beans and small pebbles. Shake it as you go to hear what it sounds like. Everyone can create their own combinations for unique sounds.

In addition to beans and pebbles, you can fill your shakers with other items such as small bells or beads. Crystal chips or stones can be charged under a full moon and add power to the shaker. Allspice increases energy while cinnamon chips draw in warmth and prosperity. A pinch of lavender promotes peace and harmony. Be careful to only add a pinch if working with herbs – too much will dull the sound of the shaker.

Once you have added all your chosen items to the shaker, seal the opening tightly and cover it with masking tape if needed to avoid an accidental opening during use. In this next step, use paint, markers, or any other crafting tools to decorate your shaker. Some materials may be more difficult to paint, so you may want to to cover the shaker in construction paper, recycled newspaper, or even masking tape before you begin the decorating process.

You can design your shaker however you like. Choose any colors, designs, or symbols you feel best align with your intentions. Add additional crafting items like feathers or pictures reinforced with a craft sealer like Mod Podge. Think about the cause you intend to raise energy for and customize your energy raising shaker to suit the theme. Preparing for a Pride festival? Add symbols you associate with Pride.

Creating your own sigils is a fantastic way to customize and create a unique design while also adding power to your new tool. Sigils are pictorial signatures designed by practitioners to aid in manifesting their intentions. When you create your own sigil, you set your intention into a symbol that is unique and special to you. Sigils are often personal, but groups with a shared purpose can utilize the same sigils to connect their intentions to each other. Sigils can be made in advance or created intuitively at the time of the working.

In addition to sigils, there are many runes from Norse traditions that could be appropriate to use in this project. Runes can be energetically activated through meditation or by closing your eyes and focusing on the intention. Multiple rules can be used at once on the same shaker. Create your own bind runes by drawing two or more runes directly on top of each other creating a unique rune symbol. Bind runes fuse the intentions of the separate runes into one symbol for increased power. If needed, perform an internet search for a chart of the runes and their meanings.

Once you have finished creating your energy raising shaker and the paint has dried, it is time to move on to part two of this working: raising the energy.

There are many ways to raise energy. Focus on your intentions of support, compassion, unity, and universal love as you dance, chant, sing, drum, and shake that shaker every which way – or rather, every *witch* way.

Build energy and add power to this working us by using music. You can use any songs that alight with your intentions and hold a positive and supportive message. Choose something that is upbeat and builds in rhythm.

Create your own customized playlist using your favorite music steaming service. If you like to use Spotify, we have created a free public playlist that can be found by searching "Community Energy Raising" featuring all these songs listed below. Use this playlist while designing the shakers as well as during the energy raising. The playlist has a slow build and increases in power with each song until the culmination of the finale, so these songs raise energy just as you do.

Community Energy Raising Playlist

- "Earth Air Fire Water" by Lila

- "Element Chant" by Spiral Rhythm

- "There is No Time" be Kellianna

- "We Are the Fire" by Ruth Barrett

- "We Are the Rising Sun" by Reclaiming

- "Elemental Children of the Earth" by Shining Wheel Pagan Chorus

- "Firebird's Child" by S.J. Tucker

- "Journey (Prelude)" by Crow Women

- "Full Height of Our Power" by Kellianna

As each song plays, allow yourself to truly feel the music. Raise energy by shaking the shaker like a rattle, dance, move in whatever way you choose. If you know the words, sing along. Sing along even if you don't know the words – many of these songs are repetitive, as they resemble chants, and are easy to learn.

If you do not have access to streaming music or if you simply want to use another method, there are chants that you can use to raise energy. Rattle the shaker to the beat of the chants as you repeat the words at least three times over. Here are three simple chants for groups to get you started:

Standing in a circle,
Hand to hand, heart to heart,
Our intentions we do impart!

We rise, we rise, we rise.
We build, we build, we build.
Together! Together! Together!

Firelight burning bright,
Our energy is full tonight!

Chanting and incantations can be use for solitary energy raising too. Here are alternatives for working by yourself:

Firelight burning bright,
My energy is full tonight!

My energy rises with the sun.
My intention builds with strength and power.

I am the change.
I am the dawning.

As your energy builds, focus on your intentions of positivity, support, compassion, and universal love, and send those intentions out into the world.

Ritual to Heal Community Divide

There is no denying there is plenty of division in our world right not, on many levels. While we tend to blame politics for the divide, the truth is, the divide is not caused by politics at all. That is a scapegoat used to not take responsibility for one's actions. The true source of the division we are seeing is a difference of ethics and belief systems clashing. One side fears losing their expected power and the control they have retained for generations, while the other side demands equality and the right to life, liberty, and the pursuit of happiness to be applied to all, not the few. We passed the lines of politics a long time ago. This isn't about how we spend tax money; for many, it has become a matter of life or death. This is not political. It is ethical.

How do we heal a community after such great division? Slowly. This type of division will never heal 100 percent, and it isn't realistic to think it will. Zealots and extremists make the world a difficult place. Denying their existence is a disservice to our communities. Ignoring problems does not make them go away. There is no easy fix to the situation we are in, but we can send healing energies to assist. While a love-filled, hate-free world may be the perfect utopia, we all know it is a bit unrealistic. What isn't unrealistic is to raise and send healing compassionate energies out into a community to help it heal.

We can apply the concept of the shadow self to society as well as to the individual. There are dark components of society which are often denied, yet need to be healed. When we work with our own shadow self, we know to listen to the expert on who we are – ourselves. When we heal our society, it is imperative we educate ourselves from reliable sources of information. Facts are verifiable. Opinions are not. Healing based on misinformation is not healing. It's continuing harm. Misinformation is dangerous and can be deadly. Be sure you understand what intentions you are working with and what energy you are sending out.

This ritual can be done on your own, but of course, getting a group of likeminded people together to help would increase the energy and power. The previous playlist can also be used here. In fact, these two rituals can be used in conjunction with one another. Use the energy raising ritual to support your cause of sending healing energies to the community.

This ritual requires a bit of advance work to prepare your altar. Find images or other representations of positive, healing, community energy. This may include things such as the scales of justice or a Pride flag, but it also may include things like a pictures of a local park filled with happy families or a playbill from a community theater group. Brainstorm examples of positive community energy. If a group will be performing this ritual, each participant should contribute with items for the altar.

Safely decorate the altar with candles. Black candles can be used to absorb negative energy and define boundaries. Blue and green candles can be added for healing energies. Brown candles are for stability, justice, and integrity. Orange candles can be included for energy, courage, pride, success, and to help open communication. Add pink candles to call upon the energies of compassion, honor, and peace. Finally, white candles represent cleansing, healing and truth. If you are working with a group, each person could be responsible for providing a specific color. You will want the altar placed in the center of your group with everyone circled around it.

Your altar will need a fireproof container to burn the incense mixture we will create. You will add self-lighting charcoal tablets to the bottom to burn your created incense. This container should have a handle so once the incense it added, you will be able to carefully pick up the container and spread the smoke all around the altar and immediate area. Again if you are working with a group, each participant should provide an item for the incense. You will combine them all together and use a mortar and pestle to grind and blend them. In a group working, each person should take a turn with the pestle.

For the incense, you may use any combination of the following dried herbs:

- Allspice for increasing energy.

- Bay laurel for strength, good fortune, and success.

- Blessed thistle for strength and vitality.

- Borage for domestic peace, courage, and to lift spirits.

- Catnip for happiness, courage, and power.

- Celandine to break oppressive chains and free depressive mindsets.

- Chamomile for peace, tranquility, healing, and reducing stress.

- Chili pepper for energy.

- Cinnamon for healing, happiness, success, love, and warmth.

- Dragon's blood to banish negative forces and to amplify the power.

- Eucalyptus for healing, cleansing, and warding off evil.

- Fennel for healing, vitality, strength, and confidence.

- Frankincense for purifying, cleansing, and manifesting.

- Hibiscus for joy and happiness.

- Hyssop for cleansing and lightening vibrations.

- Juniper berries for good health and positive energy.

- Lavender for healing, peace, and mental well being.

- Meadowsweet for peace, happiness, balance, and harmony.

- Myrrh for peace and to enhance the power of the working.

- Nettle leaf to block negativity.

- Passionflower for health, happiness, and harmony.

- Peppermint to clear negative energy and to increase vibrations.

- Sandalwood for healing, clearing away negativity, manifesting, and aiding the flow of energy.

- Witch's burr to add power.

In group work, preparing the altar and incense together allows everyone to contribute their energy to the ritual. The incense can be placed in a bowl on the altar near the fireproof container with the charcoal tablets.

Your altar should also include representations of each of the elements. Deity statues are, of course, always welcome.

When your altar is completely set up, everyone may take a place in a circle around it. Because we are working to combine energies together and amplify each other's power, each person will say the ritual in unison. No one person or voice is the leader. They are all intermingled together as one. If you are by yourself, use the "I" and "me" pronouns. If in a group, use forms of "we." For brevity, the ritual is written in first person only.

Begin by facing east and say:

> *I call upon the east and the power of air.*
> *Lend your power to this rite,*
> *Carry my energy on beams of light.*

Turn to face the south and say:

> *I call upon the south and the power of fire.*
> *Lend your power to this rite.*
> *With flames of energy throughout the night.*

Turn to face the west and say:

> *I call upon the west and the power of water.*
> *Lend your power to this rite.*
> *With waves of energy truth and right.*

Turn to face the north and say:

> *I call upon the north and the power of earth.*
> *Lend your power to this rite,*
> *Then soothe me with your grounding might.*

Turn to face the altar:

> *This energy I raise [today/tonight]*
> *I send in to the universe.*
> *I send it into my community on every scale,*
> *From my local neighborhood, to my city, my state, my country.*
> *My planet. My world. My home.*
> *We must be healed.*
> *We must heal the earth.*

Take the incense and sprinkle it gently over the lit charcoal tablets. You want enough to create a good smoke but not enough to smother the embers. (If you are doing this in a group, each person will take turns adding a pinch.) Safely pick up the container by the handle and gently move it all around the altar in front of you, spreading the smoke all around it. You may use a feather to help waft the smoke if you wish. Walk around the altar with the container as you disperse the smoke and say:

> *My energy combines with thee,*
> *To fill my community with positivity.*

Continue this chant as each person takes their turn wafting the smoke.

If you completed the energy building ritual first, you already have a nice reserve of energy to call upon. Use this chant to continue building and releasing positive energy through the air. Visualize the qualities of the herbs in their energy forms as they are carried away in the smoke. Emanate your own energy to combine with these energies. While I often visualize energy pouring out from my dominant hand, I have on occasion felt it shoot out the top of my head. You do what works for you. You do not need to worry about working the energy into a climax with one big release; you are focusing instead on a steady supply of positive, happy thoughts pumping into the universe. Continue until you feel the drain. You are giving your positive energy to the universe. You will feel drained. When you are ready to finish, say:

I give this energy willingly,
I share my hope for peace, for love, for charity.
So mote it be.

Face the north and say:

I thank the north and power of earth for your energies.
Blessings and farewell.

Face the west and say:

I thank the west and power of water for your energies.
Blessings and farewell.

Face the south and say:

I thank the south and power of fire for your energies.
Blessings and farewell.

Face the east and say:

I thank the east and power of air for your energies.
Blessings and farewell.

Always remember, if you are performing a ritual in a public location, ensure you not only have permission to use the space, but also that you leave the area as you found it, if not in better condition. Do not leave altar items out in a way for other people to label them as litter.

Ritual to Send Empathy and Compassion

No matter your political beliefs or affiliations, this nonpartisan ritual can be used to send empathy and compassion to our elected leaders and encourage them to express these traits themselves as they lead our country.

Set the scene with:

- A pink candle

- A safety pin

- A lighter of matches

- Olive oil

- Dried lavender buds

- Dried chamomile buds

Begin by preparing the pink candle. Use the safety pin to carve the word "empathy" on one side of the candle and "compassion" on the other side. Next, dress the candle using the olive oil, lavender and chamomile. Olive oil is specifically used in this candle dressing as a symbol of peace and unity. Rub the oil all over the candle, avoiding contact with the wick. The lavender and chamomile should be rolled or rubbed onto the candle to bring in peace, tranquility, healing. and harmony. (The olive oil will help little bit of flower to stick to the candle.)

When you are ready to begin, call upon your guides, deities, or the power of the universe. Set your intentions by closing your eyes and imagining a light pink energy glowing from the candle. Focus on feelings of love, empathy, compassion, peace, and unity, and send these feelings to the candle, energetically charging it with your intention. Once your candle feels appropriately charged, open your eyes. Light the wick, and speak your intention by saying:

You have been elected to a position of power,
And now I call upon you in this hour.
It is time to release selfishness and greed,
And use your power to help those in need.

As the wick burns, send the pink energy outward and confidently recite the following incantation nine times:

I send you the kindness, compassion, empathy, unity
And a desire to help improve our community.

Allow the candle to burn fully as you focus on your intention. If you are strapped for time or working with a candle too large to burn at once, then allow it to burn an hour a day, each day until the candle has been fully burned. Reaffirm your intentions every time you light the candle.

Ritual to Heal the Environment

Nature-based practices focus on working and honoring the earth. This planet is our only home, and it is important we take care of her. Pollution and deforestation wreak havoc on the environment. The land is being stripped of resources that are vital to a thriving ecosystem. There are ways to help heal the environment using both mundane and magical means. This ritual combines a metaphysical ritual with a laborious mundane task to heal the earth energetically with witchery as well as physically by planting more trees.

As this is a planting ritual, you will need access to gardening space. This ritual can be done as a tree planting project for a local community park or used to add more greenery to your own backyard. If neither of these options are accessible to you, this ritual can still be completed using a potted plant kept in your home. Another option it to repeating this ritual with multiple potted plants to give away as gifts to friends, family, neighbors, and coworkers.

The type of plant you use for this ritual is entirely up to you, but it is best to use plants that are especially known for their air purifying properties.

If using this ritual to plant greenery in public spaces, it is important to make sure that you are not planting an invasive species and that you have permission from the appropriate authorities. Be sure to choose a plant native to the local habitat to avoid damaging the local ecosystem. Your local conservation district is a great resource to get started.

Set the scene with:

- A tree sapling or other sprouted plant

- Access to soil

- Gardening tools such as a shovel or trowel

- Moon water (prepared in advance)

This ritual can be performed as a solitary or with a group. It can be repeated anytime you do some gardening or planting. Use this ritual for one potted plant, or for a hundred planted trees – whatever suits your needs.

Gather your materials, call upon your guides, and dig your hole. Place your sapling or plant in the hole. As you you fill the soil in around the roots, close your eyes and focus your intentions on growth and healing. Send this energy into the earth and the roots as you say:

Here I plant new life within the earth,
To help heal the environment and all it's worth.

Open your eyes, finish filling any spots that need to be filled, and pat the dirt three times before watering with the moon water. If you are planting more than one plant at a time, you may do the watering all at once, while saying:

Bless this earth, bless this soil,
Bless this [tree, sprout, plant] for which I toil.

Take care of the life you have planted. This ritual can be reinforced monthly by using freshly charged moon water to hydrate the plants while reciting the blessing incantation.

Remember we always want to back up our magical workings in the mundane world. What needs does your community have? What can you do to make your community a better, brighter place? No action is too big, nor too small. If we all work together to do our part, the workload becomes lighter and easier. None of us are an island unto ourselves. We live, work, play, and worship in communities with other people. We must learn how to do it in a way that ensures safety and opportunity for all.

Chapter 11
Find Your Groove

F inding your groove takes work, experimentation, creativity, and courage. Here you will find a few additional tools to assist you as you travel along your path.

Magical Threads

Ritual wear is ideal for its sacred connotations – how it makes you feel. No matter the type of clothing or accessory, ritual wear is charged with the energy and power we give it. It helps us shift from the mundane world to the ethereal realm of spirit and magic. It boosts our confidence while providing comfort. Your ritual wear and accessory collection should, if possible, be limited to ritual use only.

However, having specific items for ritualistic purposes does not mean we cannot bring magic into our mundane wardrobe.

One of my daughter's friends recently commented on an outfit I was wearing saying she couldn't wait until she was in her 50s to be able to wear something like the bohemian dress and ruffled duster I had on.

I told her, "Honey, you do not have to wait!" In fact you shouldn't wait! Find your own mundane style which still allows you to feel magical in your daily life!

Clothes that allow for comfort and energy flow won't stifle your magic. Clothes and accessories can empower you. Use them to your benefit.

Use color in your wardrobe as you would in any spell work – to protect, honor, or attract what you desire. Need courage? Dress in red. Looking to attract money? Green is your color. Wear orange to boost creativity or blue to calm anxious nerves.

Bless crystal, stone, and shell jewelry in spell or ritual work before use in your daily mundane life.

Do not hide your authentic self with passing trends. Find clothes and accessories which speak to you. Visit thrift stores or learn creative skills to personalize pieces yourself.

Natural materials such as cotton or hemp are preferred to synthetic alternatives as they contain their own natural energies while allowing our to move freely without interruptions or blockages.

I'm not saying you need to run out and buy a new wardrobe, but when you do add a new piece, be mindful of its magical potential.

You are a unique enchanting individual. Let what your wear reflect your authentic self.

Fly Your Freak Flag

Sigils, runes, the Ogham and numerous other symbols help us focus our intention and are their own source of power and energy.

Explore your creativity by designing and constructing your own flag which represents who you are.

Include as many items as you want on your flag. What do you want to highlight? What symbols, signs, and colors represent you?

For inspiration, check out the following books:

- *Signs and Symbols: An Illustrated Guide to Their Origins and Meanings* (DK Compact Culture Guides) DK 2019.

- *The Illustrated Signs and Symbols Sourcebook* by Adele Nozedar. Sterling Publishing 2015.

- *Sigil Witchery: A Witch's Guide to Crafting Magick Symbols* by Laura Tempest Zakroff. Llewellyn Publications 2018.

Use whatever mediums you wish: canvas, material, posterboard, paints, markers, crayons, die-cuts, stickers, natural items such as seeds, shells, sticks, leaves, bones, or petals. Whatever your heart desires.

Design and construct your flag to represent who you are.

Display it with pride.

Far Out Meditation

Transport yourself to a higher spiritual realm in this meditation to be at one with the universe.

If you have difficulties with visualization, do an internet image search for "galaxy" to give your mind reference points. If needed, look up images of "clouds from an airplane" too.

Set the scene with a heavy spiritual incense: myrrh, patchouli, frankincense, or any combination of these.

Create salt of sand filled bowls, or other containers, to safely burn candles in or add some other type of mood lighting such as a galaxy star projection lamp.

Wear cozy , loose fitting clothing, and lie down in a comfortable position.

If you use cannabis, getting high is perfect for this meditation and can help you more easily let go of your physical grounded self. Grind your weed with an equal amount of dried mugwort for an extra trippy effect.

Relax and imagine yourself as weightless, floating, gravity has no bounds on you. You float, rising up, higher and higher. Past the trees. Don't fight it. Allow yourself to slip away from your physical body.

Cut any strings holding you back. If you feel uncomfortable at all, take deep breaths in and out through your nose, dispelling any anxiety with your exhalation. Remind yourself it is normal to feel a vertigo like "rush" when rising into a higher state of consciousness especially as you feel yourself leaving your physical body behind. Even when this feeling is expected, it can still be unsettling and jarring. It is normal and will pass. The key is to let go and see where you go.

Float higher and higher, drifting through the clouds. Feel yourself becoming lighter and lighter, while maintaining control over your ascension. Let your consciousness lift you into outer space.

You are pure energy.

Ethereal.

Safe.

Weightless.

Open yourself to whatever messages or experiences wait for you and enjoy.

When you are ready to return, feel yourself drifting back towards earth. Your body calling your home. Gently land back on earth. Safe and sound in your personal vessel once again.

Journal Exercise

What did you learn on encounter during your meditation? What message(s) did you receive? Describe your experience.

Gimme Some Bread

Use this spell to encourage the universe to send money and positive abundance into your life.

Set the scene with:

- Dragon's blood incense

- A spell size green candle and holder

- Patchouli oil mixed with a carrier oil

- A lighter

- Hand wipes or a wet washcloth

- Create and herbal offering from a blend of leafy green plants with magical correspondences to money. Choose as many as you like from: basil, chamomile, cinquefoil, clover, dandelion, dill, fennel, fern, grape leaves, honeysuckle, lemon balm, marjoram, moonwort, mustard, peppermint, sage, sweet woodruff, and thyme. Add brambles or burrs to help the requested energy to stick to you.

- A fireproof container you can burn herbs in, or access to a bonfire. If you use a fireproof container, add self-lighting charcoal tablets to help your herbal offering burn. Due to the amount of burning, you will want to do this spell outside. Set up your altar on the ground if able, otherwise use whatever is available to you.

- Water

- A representation of earth such as dirt, sand, or salt

- A handful of cowrie shells you can carry with, such as a necklace, bracelet, belt, in your hair, or loose in a pocket or purse.

Set the incense in the east section of your altar, and the candle in the south. If you use a fireproof container and its feasible, place it in the center of your altar area.

Add representations of water in the west and earth in the north.

Place your pre-blend incense offering in a bowl and the cowrie shells in another bowl, and put in spots where there is room for them.

If you are using a bonfire, set your altar near it at a safe distance.

Light your bonfire or charcoal tablet.

When you are ready to begin, take several deep breaths, center yourself, and focus your intention.

Light the incense and say:

I call upon the power of air,
Lend your energy,
Wise and fair.

Dress the candle with the oil, working from top to bottom to draw money to you. (Keep hand wipes close by to clean oil from your fingers and be careful what you touch -face, eyes- until you get a full washing done.) Light the candle and say:

I call upon the power of fire,

Lend your energy,
Passion inspires.

Hold the water above your altar or gently sprinkle droplets of it around yourself and your altar. Say:

I call upon the power of water,
Lend your energy,
Fluid and stronger.

Hold your representation of earth or sprinkle some of it around you and your altar and say:

I call upon the power of earth,
Lend your energy,
To abundant worth.

Continue with:

I call to the universe,
Hear my petition,
Guide energies to bring
My desire to fruition.

Using a small amount, sprinkle your premade incense onto the charcoal tablet, toss it into your fire, or light it and burn in a safe manner. Say:

I beckon to the energies of the universe,
Heed my call, aid my need!
Work your magic to plant the seed.
Take these ingredients,
Combined and baked,
Bring me the bread,

I need to make!

Visualize the money you need and what you need it for. Continue adding your ingredients to the fire and repeating the incantation while it burns. Add drumming if desired. Repeat as many times as you feel it is needed.

When finished, thank the summoned energies and elements for their aid. Allow your fire to safely burn out or extinguish it.

Feelin' Foxy

Add a little spice to your lovemaking with this aphrodisiac herbal blend. It can be used with or without cannabis and may either be smoked or brewed in hot water (not boiling) by steeping 3-5 minutes.

Experiment with the following herbs to find the combination and ratios you prefer. Choose from:

- Cannabis

- Cardamom

- Cinnamon

- Clove

- Dill

- Ginger

- Ginseng

- Hibiscus

- Jasmine

- Lavender

- Nettle

- Peppermint

- Poppy

- Rosemary

- Violet

Begin your experimentation by using equal amounts of what you have on hand and enjoy making adjustments as you see fit.

Pour the blend into a glass see thru jar and hold it above your head under the light of the full moon and say:

> *I call the moon full and bright*
> *Grant me your power this magical night.*
> *Infuse this blend with ecstasy and desire,*
> *Enhance my love with passion and fire.*

Place the jar where the moon's beams will reach it either in a safe location outside or in a window.

This blend it a perfect accompaniment for sex magic.

***

Facing trauma, overcoming depression, and relearning new ways of interacting with yourself and others is quite a bit of challenging work, but finding and embracing who you are at your very core, is where the heart of magic resides. As you build your emotional power, your magical power increases too.

Chapter 12
Conclusion

Writing *Spells for Good Times* and then revamping it into *Spells for Groovy Times*, has allowed us to look within, shine a light on our own lives, and ultimately set us on new paths. While writing we reflected on our own experiences, evaluated our responses to the hardships and chaos faced in our daily lives, and discovered inspiration in the world around us. These spells and rituals have come from our own personal practices, which have helped us to heal, grow, and create brighter and more abundant lives. We are grateful for the chance to share them with you. This rewrite came at a time when I found myself needing it the most, during a time of personal turmoil centered around shattered relationships and major health care issues.

We hope *Spells for Groovy Times* has given you the tools needed to build a brighter future for yourself and those around you and in your community. We hope the spells, rituals, affirmations, meditations, prayers, and journal writings included here gave you the power and insight to build up your confidence and instill within you a sense of peace and improved self-worth.

We would like to take this opportunity to thank you for reading this book. Most importantly, we thank you for allowing us a place on your path to self-discovery and healing. We wish you luck as you continue forward on your journey.